# *the* MAP SEEKER

## *one woman's quest*

### LEAH KOTKES

ISRAEL BOOKSHOP
PUBLICATIONS

*the*
# MAP SEEKER
*one woman's quest*

## LEAH KOTKES

ISRAEL BOOKSHOP
PUBLICATIONS

Final Editor: Gila Green
Cover Design: Zippy Thumim
Page Layout and Design: Eden Chachamtzedek

Published by:
Israel Bookshop Publications
501 Prospect Street
Lakewood, NJ 08701

Tel: (732) 901-3009
Fax: (732) 901-4012
www.israelbookshoppublications.com
info@israelbookshoppublications.com

*Printed in the United States of America*

**Rabbi CHAIM P. SCHEINBERG**

Rosh Hayeshiva "TORAH ORE"

and Morah Hora'ah of Kiryat Mattersdorf

הרב חיים פינחס שיינברג

ראש ישיבת "תורה אור"

ומורה הוראה דקרית מטרסדורף

בס"ד

January 25, 2009/ 29 Tevet 5769

I have known Mrs. Leah Kotkes since 1993, and she is a frequent visitor to our home.

I personally asked Mrs. Kotkes to pen her journey to *Yiddishkeit* into a published book and with my blessings she has completed it.

As in all of her writings, Mrs. Kotkes has succeeded in capturing the essence of faith with this book. She has presented her journey with clarity and has much *chizuk* and inspiration to offer the English speaking reader. This book has a most relevant message in today's times when so many are in need of a true tale of perseverance and vision in order for them to follow Hashem's path and to know Him.

It is my hope and prayer that from between the pages of this book thousands of people will come closer to Hashem and His Torah.

רחוב פנים מאירות 2, ירושלים, ת.ד. 6979, טל. 537–1513 (02), ישראל

2 Panim Meirot St., Jerusalem, P.O.B. 6979, Tel. (02) 537-1513, Israel

PRAISE FOR *The Map Seeker*

S ome people live according to an erroneous ideology, but many
more people have no ideology at all, and go through the motions
of life unmotivated by an ultimate purpose. In *The Map Seeker*, Leah
Kotkes relates her personal journey, finding her way to the meaning-
fulness of Torah living. Mrs. Kotkes shares with us the experiences
that led her to the discovery of the beauty of a Torah life.

*Rabbi Abraham Twerski M.D.*
*Psychologist, noted writer and lecturer*

B rilliantly titled, *The Map Seeker* is a literary feast for mind and
soul. Leah Kotkes, a seasoned writer, describes an astonishing
journey toward a life of truth founded upon authentic Judaism in a
way that will inspire readers to find and create their own maps toward
G-d. More than other memoirs about a return to observance, this
work shimmers with vivid details and powerfully evoked personages
of great religious conviction. To her credit, Leah Kotkes has not spared
the reader the pain or the detours that mark the inner travels of the
map seeker. Here we find hard-earned wisdom powerfully conveyed.

*Vera Schwarcz, Director of the Freeman Center for East Asian Stud-*
*ies at Wesleyan University, CT, is the author of the prize-winning study*
*"Bridge Across Broken Time: Chinese and Jewish Cultural Memory."*

T hat Leah Kotkes wrote "The Map Seeker," the riveting story of
her personal quest for fulfillment, is not surprising, since it is
through writing that she has been sharing her inner self with other
women as a published feature writer and author. What amazes me is
her courage in not hiding behind a pen-name, but rather connecting
to her readers in a most honest, open manner, "from the heart — to
the heart," a formula guaranteed to touch hearts and change lives.

*Sarah Birnhack, Brooklyn, New York*

Leah Kotkes's deeply-felt memoir is the story of one woman's courageous decisions to make pivotal changes in her inner and outer life. Her gripping account takes the reader along through her aspirations, frustrations, and ultimately finding her true place. The author's sincerity and passion to live a life of truth is bound to move any reader.

*Sara Yoheved Rigler,*
*Author of best selling biography "Holy Woman"*

Leah Kotkes is a survivor of many life ordeals. She bravely and exquisitely writes about how she overcame each one in *The Map Seeker: One Woman's Quest.* Readers will notice how, at every life stage, Leah yearns to discover new worlds. Yet her most fantastic journey is within the world of her own consciousness. She lets us in on her thoughts, dreams and even what actions she is willing to take to achieve her soul's truest desires.

This memoir is a must read for every career girl — past and present.

*Heather Dean Haas, Journalist and author of upcoming memoir,*
*"For the Love of G-d: My Extraordinary Career as a*
*Celebrity Interviewer & Why I Left It"*

I read *The Map Seeker*; I was deeply moved. I followed Leak Kotkes wherever her voice gracefully took me along her path through life. Her book is a true journey of the soul; I thank her for letting me read it. The book is a most precious one.

*Nechama Bornstein, Reader, originally from*
*Copenhagen, now living in Jerusalem*

Leah Kotkes's memoir is about a woman's journey towards the truth and the claim that she makes on her spiritual heritage. Leah takes us scene by scene through the trials that forced her to forge a new identity and helped her begin to fulfill her potential.

Leah's honesty with herself and her readers compels us to see beyond her words and glean from her experiences. This helps to set each one of us on the path of her own search for truth.

*Rhona Lewis, freelance writer,*
*originally from Kenya, now living in Israel*

# In Memory Of

My beloved Grandma, Mrs. Rose Shawdon (1906 — 1996)

My beloved Rebbetzin, Raichel Horowitz (1919 — 2002)
The first wife of Grand Rabbi Levi Yitzchak Horowitz,
the Bostoner Rebbe *shlit"a*

# Dedication

For my husband: thank you for being you so I can be me and for the space in between which is our life, our children and our work for Klal Yisrael.

For my beloved children: so you will understand who I was and appreciate what I tried to become for the sake of your future in Klal Yisrael in Eretz Yisrael.

For my readers: I write for you; thank you for your loyalty.

A few words of appreciation to: my Creator and Tatty in *Shamayim:* thank You for being with me from the beginning and giving me hope that You will be there until the end. I am never alone because You are always with me.

Harav Chaim Pinchas Scheinberg *shlit"a*: thank you, my dear Rav, for telling me to write this book during Chanukah 2000, for constantly prompting me to do so whenever I saw you and for your wise counsel throughout the years it took me to complete this manuscript.

For my mother, father and brother: for being patient when you didn't understand and trying to be patient when you did.

Grand Rabbi Levi Yitzchak Horowitz, the Bostoner Rebbe *shlit"a*, and the Rabbanit: thank you for opening your home and your heart to our family; thank for your words of encouragement, your *brachos* and your belief in my abilities on behalf of Jewish women.

Rabbi Dovid Gottlieb *shlit"a*: if it had not been for your ability to break down the fences in my mind and to help me see what must be done immediately, I would not have begun a new lifelong journey.

To my mentors who helped lay the foundation for my new life dedicated to Torah and mitzvos, Rabbi Rashi and Ruthie Simon, Rabbi Yisroel and Julie Roll: thank you for your time, your counsel, and your example.

Dvora Simon: thank you for listening and for being the most thoughtful and kind friend anyone could wish for.

Leah Mark: for your friendship, your steadfast strength and the benefit of your brilliant, beautiful mind.

Rebbetzin Rivka Misselman: the door is always open, the heart is ready to listen, the mind is always ready with good advice, the hands are always ready to do *chessed*.

Rebbetzin Yehudit Soloveitchik: thank you for telling me you loved me at the right time in my life. Your words rekindled my love for life.

R' Aryeh: thank you for being a great source of support during the past year. Your benevolence has made the future brighter.

Rabbi Daniel Yaakov Travis: you lit the candle in the dark, led the way out, and showed me a way forward. Thank you.

To my past and current editors: Chavi Ernster, Faigel Safran and today, Mrs. Ruth Lichtenstein, my editor-in-chief, Sarah Birnhack, and the staff at *Binah* Magazine; your support enables me to fulfill my dream of writing for Klal Yisrael.

To Ayalah Haas: a new friend, a new guiding light, a very special *neshamah* who refined my story for every woman. Thank you.

To my publisher, Moshe Kaufman and his staff at Israel Bookshop and Gila Green, my final editor: you both came into my life in 2008 and have helped me actualize a vision of an idea; thank you most sincerely for supporting my story, my Rav's aspiration for me and my lifework, that of writing for the reader.

To every woman who has extended a kind word and a gesture of friendship to me: thank you.

# Contents

# Note to the Reader

The names of some of the people in this book have been changed to honor privacy. The words and the stories linked to these people have been shortened and carefully presented for the sake of the goals of this memoir.

In this book there may be words that are not familiar to you. I want you to feel comfortable in the pages of my memoir which was written for you. If you come across one of these unfamiliar words please kindly turn to the glossary on page 295; it was created for you to introduce you to the world of words that I use today.

Forgive me for not telling you all the chapters of my life; I had to make a choice between what to share and what to keep private. My sincere hope is that there is enough in this memoir to give the best picture possible of my life of faith which I pray will be an inspiration for your own life.

# *Preface*

Memoir — snapshots out of a lifetime — is a relatively new genre for me, a seasoned published writer for seven years and an aspiring writer from a young age. But I am coming to love this genre which allows me to share chapters of my life in a purposeful, creative way without telling the whole story, which is too long to record in one book and too deeply personal to tell all.

When writing this memoir, the past and the present merged and then separated as I tried to put into words how it was then and how it is for me today looking back on the past. It is impossible to remember all the details of the past and to relate to all the new feelings that came up when writing this memoir. I was patient with myself when I wrote this book that starts when I was a child of seven and takes the reader on the pathway I took towards a life of faith. I pray you will be patient with me as I try to tell you the story that I feel must be shared and the story my spiritual advisor has been asking me to write for nine years. Finally, I am reaching his goal and also my own and the feeling is gratifying.

Leah Kotkes
Jerusalem
Israel

PART ONE

# *Beyond Hendon*

# 1

*Age Seven, 1970*

The house is big, quiet — the carpet dark brown; I don't like the color, it's not beautiful to me, so when I walk downstairs to the pretty mint green breakfast room I lift my head up.

In the breakfast room I look out on the garden; it's waiting for me, like it is every morning. Dusty, my black cat, purrs at my ankle. Tasha, our small black and white Shih Tzu dog, sits by my feet, nose pressed on the glass door.

The patio tiles are cool on my bare feet, in seconds they are drenched in dew, as I make my way across the grass. The morning air is fresh, the sky is brightening into a lovely blue. The trees, the shrubs, the rose bushes, the flowers — each one of nature's gifts beckons me.

First I open my rabbit's cage. Snowball dances on his paws, pulling at the bars with his little pink mouth. He jumps out. All three animals say "good morning" to each other while I wander off to say "good morning" to my beloved garden.

I love the silence of the morning, private time with G-d, whom I feel everywhere; I love Him for everything, from being in my life, for making the sun shine, the flowers grow, for giving me my pets, to watching over me in my family home, where I feel lonely most of the time until I remember He is there with me.

If I get down to the garden early enough I take my camera to photograph something interesting like a pretty rose, some lovely fruit, a "garden visitor" — a hedgehog, a caterpillar, or a bird.

I check my watch, chase Snowball to put him back in his cage and run upstairs to prepare for school. It's *Weetabix* and milk for breakfast every day, heated up in the microwave with a sprinkling of sugar — delicious.

I know where everything is in the house; Mum has trained me well. I woke myself, made my bed and dressed myself.

Now, I eat carefully, not wanting to dirty my clean clothes. Dad left over an hour ago; I heard the garage doors, the sound of the big engine disappearing down the street. Mum and my brother of four and a half are asleep in their rooms.

I glance often at my watch; I feel anxious. I rush to finish by sipping the milk. I put on my coat, take my bag, go out the front door, returning twice to double check I shut it properly so nobody can get in.

I walk quickly on the left side of the street; I don't want to be late — I won't be — I never am, I'm always early; "Better to be early than late," say Mum and Dad.

At 7:20 A.M. the street's sleepy and empty. At the corner there's an apartment block with a high staircase. I see Mrs. Thomas coming down, carefully holding the rail with one hand and her walking stick in the other. I slow down, waiting at the bottom and announce myself as her shoe touches the pavement. She says she is happy I am here and takes my arm. Mrs. Thomas is the same height as me; I'm pretty tall for my age. People say it's because Dad's tall.

As we walk we talk; there is a rhythm in our stride. Sometimes it feels like I am walking alone when I am with her because we walk in a similar way. She tells me her daughter brought over home-baked biscuits, and asks me over later to get some.

On the main road cars, buses, motorbikes pass by in both directions. We make our way past the traffic lights to the main line station and then stop at a shop for Mrs. Thomas. She pats my hand and says, "Goodbye little angel; remember to come later for some biscuits." Then she disappears inside.

Mrs. Thomas is the only blind old woman I know. I want to help her; I know it is important to help everyone; Mummy does and I want to also. I met Mrs. Thomas when she dropped her walking stick and asked out loud if someone could help. We have been friends for a long time.

I walk up the hill from the station. I look into the faces of the people walking past me; they look the same, they wear dark clothes, none are smiling. This bothers me; perhaps I look like them also. I don't want to. I smile at them even though I don't know them.

I stop at the top of the hill to look at the four cedar trees in the island in the middle of the road. They are gigantic. Their bare trunks go up a long way until a wide umbrella-shape of branches and leaves. Every day I admire the trees — there is something about them that I like.

The school cleaner is at the top of the steps when I arrive half an hour later.

"A good morning to you," says the happy man with a nod. He is wearing a cardigan with patched elbows, holding a long wooden mop. Fluffy white water foams around his rubber boots; a white river runs down each step. I smile at him; he is cleaning our school, and I appreciate that.

When the steps are clear I go inside, down the long corridor. The floor is shiny; it smells of cleaning liquid. My classroom is empty.

Walking around, I'm not worried. The headmistress is here; I see the light on in her window. Soon she'll come out and say,

"Good morning" in her singsong voice, then my friends will arrive, and we'll play until Mrs. Morgan comes. She's lovely; I can't wait to see her.

I watch the clock at school; at three o'clock Mum will pick me up in her car. We'll go shopping or go home. If we go shopping, I'll pack the boxes in the shop and put the things away in the kitchen.

As soon as Mum drives up to our house I see Dusty sitting in the bay window. When Mum opens the front door, Dusty's already there. She rubs against my ankle, then follows me around the house. Tasha follows Dusty; it's really funny when she does this. When I let Snowball out of his cage, after his runabout he'll follow Dusty and Tasha upstairs to my room where I do my homework. When I see the three of them waiting on the carpet for me to finish, I can't help laughing. They are a funny bunch of "friends" I know, but I love them dearly.

I found Dusty in the outhouse on the patio when we moved in. The week-old kitten was meowing loudly and covered in dust. I fed her with a Baby-Tiny-Tears bottle and held her often. I became her mummy. She follows me everywhere, even when I go for a walk in the street.

My brother is too little to be my friend; he's mostly with Mummy, but I don't mind. I have my pets and a few school friends I like very much.

I don't remember so much about my early childhood except for house guests, our visits to other people's homes and sad things like going to funerals.

I am jumping to a new memory when I was eight. On the weekends our house is quiet. It's quiet most of the time during the week also. It only gets noisy when my parents' friends come to visit or for dinner parties. After school and on weekends I like to be in my bedroom at my desk writing stories and drawing them out. I don't read them to anyone because maybe I might be laughed at.

Today, it's Sunday afternoon, the day Uncle Dave and Aunty Hetty usually come, after we've driven down to see my grandparents in Stamford Hill. Aunty Hetty is grandma's eldest sister. Aunty Lily is the youngest. Daddy is Aunty Hetty's nephew.

I don't hear the doorbell upstairs. I only know when someone's arrived when Mum or Dad call me.

I've been working on a children's story for some time now. It's about a girl my age, who befriends a rabbit. This rabbit doesn't have a toothbrush; this bothers the little girl who thinks it's important for him to brush his big teeth.

"Everyone has to brush their teeth," the little girl tells him. "How will you have a nice smile if you don't brush your teeth? How will you eat if your teeth are bad?"

The little girl decides to take the rabbit through Toothbrush Wood to ask the Toothbrush King for a toothbrush for the rabbit and his friends.

I am drawing a picture of the little girl and the rabbit walking through Toothbrush Wood. There's a knock at my door. Aunty Hetty comes in. She's smaller than I am and to me she is birdlike. Her eyes look shocked like a barn owl; her tummy is round and puffed out like a robin redbreast. Her legs are thin and long like a flamingo. Her face widens when she smiles like a black bird with his mouth open, waiting for food.

She stands by my desk, looks down at my picture and asks me what I am doing. I blush. She puts her small hand on my shoulder. I look up into her curious face. Her eyes turn kind and friendly. I decide to tell her the story of the Toothbrush King and how he gives each rabbit a toothbrush so the rabbits have clean teeth and nice smiles.

"This is a lovely story. A very good idea. Well done," says Auntie Hetty.

"I love it also. Do you really like it?"

She nods and pats my shoulder again.

"Come down and see Uncle Dave. He has something for you."

I put down my coloring pencil and follow her downstairs; Dusty comes also.

Uncle Dave is sitting in the velvety brown lounge with my father. He waves at me and smiles. I stand at the opposite end of the room beside Aunty Hetty.

"Come here, Vanessa," he says, holding out his hand. "This is for you. Buy yourself something you like."

Uncle Dave puts a coin in my palm. The fifty-pence piece feels cold. I look at my father on the other couch, who is looking at me.

"Thank you Uncle Dave."

I leave the room, close the door behind me, go back upstairs to put the money in a safe place. Then I stand by the window overlooking our garden and all the gardens in our street, resting my head on the glass and letting my eyes wander over the view and the grey winter sky. The glass is cold. There's not much else to do today. Soon it will be bedtime, then time to return to school.

# 2

I didn't imagine I would be where I am right now when I was a young child. What I hoped, by the time I was eight years old, was that one day I would be a writer and someone that does special things with words and pictures — and thank G-d I do that today in my work as a writer, editor and publisher.

But I never dreamed one day I would be living in Eretz Yisrael, I would be *shomeret* Torah and *mitzvos*, that I would be a wife to a rabbi and Torah scholar and a mother to four children.

As a child I yearned for a world more appropriate for me beyond our family home in Hendon. I prayed for a place where I belonged, where I would be appreciated, where I could be me. I hoped this with all my young heart, but I had no idea *where* it was or *how* I would get there.

Hendon, in North West London, England, is where we moved in 1968 when I was five. We lived in Edgware, a borough in Middlesex beforehand. I lived in Hendon until I was twenty-five years old. This home was a base from which I developed a second life, becoming an industrious and worldly person. I was one type of person in our family home and quite another person in the world at large.

I lived at home until I was twenty-five because it was convenient — materially — and because I didn't want to live alone. At eighteen, when I started working, my life outside the house was so challenging and demanding, home, my familiar bedroom particularly, was a safe haven at the end of a very long work day or travel overseas.

Our home, a large detached house with a one-acre garden, was kept clean and ordered by home-help. Mum didn't work outside the home but worked diligently inside managing the helpers with kindness and clear vision. My father gradually became financially comfortable after starting out with very little in his early twenties. "Not more than a few pounds in his pocket," according to my mother. "That didn't bother me," said Mummy one time. "I married for love."

The personality of our family home mirrored that of my parents' lives. Dad, a menswear clothing manufacturer, worked long hours, traveled overseas, spoke mostly shop talk or *Financial Times*-speak during meals, after which he rejuvenated in silence over a newspaper or a television documentary in the garden room until retiring. Some weeknights my parents went out with their friends leaving me and my brother with an *au pair* or a babysitter.

Dad, a slender well-groomed man of 6 foot 2 with a great sense of style, was mostly "present" for me and my brother on Sundays, when we invariably went for leisurely family walks to Kenwood House, one of my favorite places, a magnificent stately home with an art gallery, grandiose library and a forest-edged lake near Hampstead Heath. Afterwards, we usually made the forty-minute drive to visit my Mum and Dad's parents, all of whom lived in Stamford Hill — in relatively simple, small lodgings — except my paternal grandfather, who died when my father was in his early twenties.

From Monday to Friday, Mum, English-born like my father, with a vivacious personality and a beloved devotion to her girlfriends and her parents, looked after me and my brother with a sense of strictness and high expectations, but always with a large helping of good humor. Music turned up, she often laughed and danced around the kitchen with my brother who was two and half years my junior. When he was eight, he was sent to a different school from me and then on to a top English-style Christian all-boys boarding school at age eleven (many Jewish boys were sent there who became his friends and are still his friends today). He lived away from home until he was sixteen, coming home every other weekend. Mum missed my brother very much. Often I accompanied her to visit him on weekdays, waiting in the car when she delivered him treats.

On Saturday afternoons, Dad and his friends and my brother, when he was home from school, went to watch their football team play at Tottenham Hotspur, while I accompanied Mum on a shopping spree. We were usually successful thanks to Mum's perseverance and excellent taste.

Summers my family stayed close to home, doing nothing particularly special. When school finished I counted the days until school started up so I would have company and my day would have some sort of structure and purpose. I didn't like school, but at least I had something to do there. I was often lonely and bored at home. My parents' closest friends had only boys — my brother always had someone to play with. I sometimes visited school girlfriends, but they mostly went away in the summer when we stayed in England, so I stayed home writing, drawing, painting, listening to music and playing with my pets, helping Mum with errands or visiting my grandparents.

But as soon as the chilly winds of winter arrived, usually in early October, my parents were already preparing for their escape to the sun and a smile was rising on my face. Our family spent every winter at a lovely hotel somewhere in the Mediterranean: Canary Islands, Italy or Israel. Sometimes we were with a group of my parents' friends and their children, again mostly boys, so I usually spent time with Mum and her girlfriends, unless I met a new friend of my own age. The best part of these winter holidays was swimming outdoors under the blue skies and sailing on lovely boats, one of my father's favorite pastimes.

Whatever the time of year, my favorite pastime was being in our garden in Hendon, which my father had surrounded in fir trees for privacy.

I developed a love of nature through my relationship with the garden. I could often be found marveling at the blooming seasons, especially spring when the rose bushes, fruit trees and sprawling, bountiful blackberry bush were at their best and most beautiful.

Spring, summer, autumn, winter — any time of day or night — you could find me in our garden, walking barefoot in the dew, watching the escalating and diminishing moon, monitoring the development of every flower, shrub and tree, picking blackberries and apples (which Mum made into scrumptious blackberry and apple pie), planting cherry pits, or watering the fir trees. Even in my winter coat I sat in a garden chair contemplating life and talking to G-d.

I felt G-d's closeness in my life from an early age: I saw Him in nature. His reliability comforted me, His presence awed me. I chatted to Him whenever I was alone. I tried to write to Him but someone once read my journal. From that day on I was private about my relationship with G-d; it was precious, something of my own.

# 3

*Age Ten, 1973*

I long for the days when it is my turn to visit Cheryl Wolfson's home after school. Cheryl and I are inseparable. We spend the afternoon in the piano room, at the bottom of the garden.

Aside from the Steinberg piano and stool there is a cozy armchair to snuggle into. Top to bottom shelves of interesting books line one wall. The fragrance of jasmine perfumes the room on late summer days. Wrapped in winter coats, scarves and warm boots, we are too engrossed to notice the winter cold.

Watching Cheryl's hands glide across the keys, I semi-close my eyes and imagine myself playing. A small smile shapes my lips; I love piano music, I love being in this room, I love my friend for letting me come to her home.

"Let's go to tea."

The words linger while Cheryl races out the door and up the stepping stone path through the garden to the house. I'm not in a rush. I sit on the stool. After arranging my skirt and aligning my posture I scrunch my fists, stretching out my hands, then exercise my fingers by bringing them up and down in a wave motion four or five times. I then place their warm tips on the cool ivory and take a deep breath.

"If only I knew how," I say, a tear running down my face.

I let my fingers free-dance, enjoying the illusion. This time, Cheryl returns and is leaning on the doorframe. She claps when I complete my "performance."

"One day," I dream, but I don't finish my sentence.

The kitchen smells delicious. Fresh tomato sauce and steaming spaghetti topped with grated cheese have been served into colorful ceramic dishes on the table, which is covered with a yellow cotton cloth that matches the napkins.

Everyone takes their regular place, including me. At the round table sit Cheryl's parents and her younger sister.

"The theme tonight will be characters from Charles Dickens," announces Mr. Wolfson; Cheryl's father makes an excellent tea-time quiz mediator.

Some years later, I am sitting in the back of the car as it glides along the road. People stop and stare. The racing green Rolls Royce is stunning, a beautiful piece of craftsmanship. Inside the car the mood is somber. Mum and Dad are silent. My mind is speeding. I hope I will know what to do. Dad parks the car with calculated ease. He is an excellent driver. We get out. I walk behind my parents. People are overflowing out of Cheryl's house into the garden, onto the pavement. Everyone is waiting.

A big black car moves down the street towards the Wolfsons' house. The mourners hush and then disperse into their own cars. A convoy follows the black leader. The convoy continues on foot behind the men carrying the coffin. Cheryl's father is lowered into the hole in the ground. I watch the box disappear down, down, down and start crying. This is going to happen to me one day; I don't want it to. Mrs. Wolfson and her daughters are crying very loudly. Everyone is crying. I can't believe what is happening. Mr. Wolfson is dead; he drowned.

Back in the house Mrs. Wolfson tells the story to my parents, her friends from club days, when they were fourteen. Cheryl is staring into space. I haven't seen her since I started a different school when we were eleven. I feel awkward. I hate death and funerals; this isn't my first funeral but it is my first visit to a *shivah* house.

The visitors mingle. The men talk business. Mrs. Wolfson holds a china teacup, her little finger rising in the air. She turns her head to chat with a group of girlfriends who have edged their way forward. I look around the room. Everyone is carrying on as if nothing has changed; they look normal, except Cheryl. She looks like she has seen a ghost. Her eyes are stuck open wide and her face is whitish, not olive-skinned like me. She is jittery, wringing her hands in her lap, over and over and over again.

"Cheryl," I gasp, unable to get my words out.

"Cheryl," I repeat. I want to tell her I have fond memories of her father. He was a fun, kind person. How can it be he is gone?

I want to say: "Cheryl, what can I do for you?" I reach out to touch her hand but it retracts like a frightened kitten. Cheryl stares past me. "Leave me alone. You can't help me. I hate G-d. He took my father."

I hadn't thought about G-d.

I look at the silver candlesticks on the shelf behind Cheryl's head. I look into the dancing flames. I remember tea quizzes and my seat at the Wolfsons' kitchen table. Mr. Wolfson's encouraging words and Mrs. Wolfson's sunny smile after school appear in my mind.

Why did G-d take Mr. Wolfson away? Where is G-d now? What is Cheryl going to do?

# 4

As far back as I can recall, Mum and Dad did not make small "unnecessary" talk with my brother and me. They certainly did not open a conversation with us about G-d or religion or anything so personal. They kept an intimate dialogue with their close friends from Jewish Club Days in Stamford Hill and didn't discuss much of anything with us unless it was technical or instructional. In our home, it was expected behavior for children to be seen and not heard. Respect and obedience were the norm; I didn't feel my voice was of great importance. I felt this mostly when I stepped out of line — sometimes from frustration, sometimes when I felt I was misrepresented, often from a lack of knowing where the line started and ended.

University for me and my brother was not on Dad's agenda. He frequently told me how he had struggled as a youngster; he had to forego a higher education as a teenager to help support his family. My brother and I were expected to go to work, not to university to develop career prospects through an education. Therefore, after I graduated from high school at sixteen, which was the norm in England in the 1970's, I took two local one-year college courses in business studies and art and design and went about looking for a job.

When my brother was seventeen, he became an apprentice in a highly respected city stock broking firm, owned by my father's best friend.

# 5

*Age Eighteen, 1982*

From a young age I accompanied Dad to menswear trade fashion shows where he presented his clothing collection to shop and department store buyers. I loved anything to do with style by the time I was a teenager; I read fashion magazines, liked to dress well, and felt at home in Dad's world. I even had a Saturday job in a designer menswear store which Dad arranged so I could have my own pocket money. "With a business course and an art and design course behind you and your father's business sense, you should be able to get any job you like," said Mum, ever the optimist.

But where should I start looking for a job? I didn't know what to do. All I knew was that there were unsaid expectations; I had to succeed.

In a women's magazine, I read about a successful fashion publicist, who was also a successful sales agent for women's wear designer labels. It took me two weeks to pluck up the courage to phone her.

I wore something classic and tailored to the meeting and took along my black portfolio. The publicist looked through my style reports and photographs of the fashion capitals I had visited so far — New York, Paris, Florence — trips I had made with friends.

"Do you want to be a fashion writer or a publicist or sales person? Make up your mind," she said, her hair cascading down the back of her suede jacket.

I wanted to trust her with my dream — I really wanted to be a writer — but I held my tongue. I had no real expertise, just a desire, really a passion, to write stories, to report and record what I had seen, to combine my love of writing and photography, to capture something exciting and share it with others; to do something worthy that would be regarded as worthy by others.

The publicist employed me. I rushed home with a job and with hopes for great things to come. Within a year I was head-hunted by the most respected fashion PR consultant in London and from there I progressed speedily up the management ladder by helping my clients gain high-profile coverage and introductions in the media. One of my first clients was John Galliano, then fresh out of college and today the house designer at Dior.

I recall a great day three years into my career: I am flying to Milan and I am very excited. At the hotel I mingle with the fashion elite: editors, writers and buyers. The *Max Mara* fashion show is everything I imagined it would be. I have been wearing this Italian brand name exclusively for years, and now I am seeing the new collection on the runway for the first time.

I'm in my element. I'm in one of the leading designer fashion capitals of the world and I have an exciting job. What more could I want?

I am beyond Hendon at last. I am doing something fantastically thrilling with my life. I am very grateful for the opportunity to work hard to advance in my profession, to emulate my peers who I highly respect, to learn from the masters of the field of my expertise. Hard work equals results, equals promotion, equals more recognition, equals more money and a company car and perks. The winning equation of life for a twenty-something girl with no university degree, who is determined to win career recognition and people's approval and respect.

# 6

The leap from a sheltered Jewish home in North West London into an entrepreneurial business arena was a culture shock; I was initially intimidated by the demands and competitiveness of the workplace and my new peers and colleagues.

In most respects Dad had prepared me well. I was business-oriented, but the interfacing with all different types of people of all ages and backgrounds took time to master. I was naïve and inexperienced in interpersonal relationships and lacking in a greater knowledge of my specialist field. But I had no choice but to persevere. I was expected to succeed — just like my brother — regardless of my gender.

In hindsight, I see that Dad's outlook worked very well for my brother, but long-term it wasn't suitable for me, who often felt Dad may have preferred me to be a boy. I don't feel he spoke to me like a girl but rather raised me with masculine expectations: to earn money, to be financially independent, to succeed.

As I progressed in my occupation, I grew restless every few years, and, not knowing why, hopped from one job to another and from one rung on the ladder up to the next in the quest for something more important, more satisfying, and more fabulous. Never did I realize (at least not until ten years later) that work alone cannot fulfill all of a person's needs and cannot offer what a Jewish girl's destiny entails.

My career as a PR and marketing expert-in-training took me on travels around England, to New York and to many cities in Europe, fueling my desire to see the world and experience its cultures, an interest that had begun as a visually-orientated youngster poring over *National Geographic* and travel magazines.

It was on these business travels that I started contemplating life; the luxury hours of quiet motion affords a traveler the privilege of exploring inner worlds through thinking, journal writing and reading.

Alone with my thoughts I dreamt big dreams and visualized all sorts of possibilities — personal and professional. I also eventually arrived at the startling conclusion that the life I was living was bringing me no peace of mind or real satisfaction.

The further afield I traveled — eventually on personal travels — the more spiritually inclined people I met, the more I realized how far I was from being in touch with my true self and my true needs. I was not happy with myself and my choices. I was becoming increasingly bored with professional obligations; I was frustrated with myself and the limitations of my social and work parameters. I was sure there was more to life and living than what I knew. I was sure there was a more satisfying way to live in the world, and others who had discovered it already. By the time I got to my mid-twenties I felt like a robot, not a human being. Yet, something deep inside of me, an unknown consciousness, spurred me onwards toward frequent exploratory travels, prompting my curious personality in search of something that I hoped existed but had yet to find. It was something I could not name. I became a seeker without a map or any clue as to how to find what I was looking for.

7

*Age Twenty-five, 1989*

I am living in a studio apartment, near Regents Park, Central London. Six months ago my father sold our family home in Hendon and purchased three apartments — for him and Mum, me and my brother.

The gap between idea and reality can be vast. The shock of living alone disturbs me terribly — overnight I hate living alone, I hate this apartment, I hate what has happened. I am no longer free. I am no longer living in a large house. I no longer have my personal freedom. I feel chained to the responsibility of this tiny, one-room bed-sit with a bathroom, walk-through kitchen and no amenities except a mini-bar fridge and a two-ring stove top. My old friends are forty-five minutes away by car. My monthly mortgage payments are constraining my social spending. I feel like I am suffocating.

A prestigious London address with a twenty-four-hour porter appealed to my parents, who assured me that living a ten-minute drive from work would be advantageous. While I agreed, the reality was humiliating and depressing.

I schlep dirty laundry to the local launderette and sit with the local foreign immigrants waiting for the cycle to end. In the morning I look out onto a brick wall, the view from the sole window, and have started to pace the 12 foot by 12 foot bed-sit by nightfall, planning my break out.

I had always harbored the thought that it was impossible

39

G-d could put man in this world without some sort of map. This thought hounded me the first few weeks in my new home simply because I felt lost, like I had taken the wrong path and didn't know what to do next.

I talked through my predicament with Angelica one Sunday when we were talking on the phone. My social life in central London was my only respite. Angelica was a business associate who had become a dear friend. She lived alone in a fashionable Chelsea two-storey apartment with a garden. We saw each other on weekends and spoke frequently on the phone.

"We have to change our lives; this is not the way to live," I said. "We can't go on like this forever. I certainly don't want to live in this apartment for the rest of my life and I certainly don't want to come home to an empty apartment every night."

"Well, that's the way it is right now, so you're going to have to accept it, just like I do," said Angelica.

"I don't want to. I want to sell as soon as possible, rent for while and start traveling more. I want to find a better way to live, a different way to live. I won't find what I'm looking for in England."

"This is it, get used to it. There is no other way," said Angelica, laughing.

"No. Not for me. I have to find another way but I don't know where to start. How could G-d have put me down here without a guidebook?" I said.

"G-d did that to all of us. Life is about writing your own guide-book," Angelica said.

"I cannot believe it. It would take a lifetime to work out how to manage in this world. There has to be another way."

"This is it, kiddo," said Angelica, suggesting we meet for lunch in an hour and a half.

I politely bowed out, and had a good cry while taking a long walk through Regents Park, one of my favorite parks, that had a lake, a rose garden and zoo.

It was raining as I made my way towards London Zoo. Standing before the giraffe house I thought how lucky the giraffe is; this is the way he looks, this is the way he lives, this is what is expected of him.

"But I am not a giraffe," I said to the void of wet weather. "I have free will. I can choose, but what should I choose?"

I sat on a bench in the empty zoo and closed my eyes and let my tears mingle with the raindrops. The silence absorbed my sobbing.

As I walked home, drenched and despondent, I replayed my conversation with Angelica. How could it be? Surely she's got it wrong.

# 8

Shortly after this walk in the zoo, I asked my parents to sell my apartment. I told them I didn't want the obligation and wanted to rent with another girl and change my profession. It was like I had dropped a bomb. Dad looked at me completely shell-shocked.

"A daughter of mine, rent? You're not serious are you?" he said.

"After everything we've done for you. How could you?" said my mother.

Without much explanation, I insisted on freedom from the home and lifestyle that was overwhelming me. Luck was on my side; Dad sold the apartment immediately, without a loss, and I lived with my parents for a few months until I found a rented apartment in one of London's most stylish literary neighborhoods, Little Venice, Maida Vale. My landlady was the editor of Penguin's Children's Puffin Books. I was so happy to be surrounded by her frequent and fascinating guests in her cozy, friendly home.

My one-year contract as a marketing director of a Royal Warrant company was coming to a close. I had spent a year promoting a luxury brand and had gained highly successful results, but I felt this work was becoming less than desirable to me; while my clients came closer to their targets, I was no closer to becoming the person I wanted to be but still could not see. Now that I was free of large financial responsibilities I was determined to have a fresh start and finally pursue my childhood dream.

Every day for six weeks I popped into the personnel office at a television news company that was recognized worldwide for fine journalism and excellence in reporting. I asked for a job, any job. I wanted to work my way up and become a writer. I wanted to work in a visual medium that was respected by the masses, that was worthy, that recorded and reported something of significance.

My daily perseverance paid off with a job offer to work as personal assistant to the news editor in the newsroom at Independent Television News (ITN); a job where I could see the inner workings of a news story in the making, where I could learn a journalist's disciplines, where I could become whomever I wanted to be without the past pulling me back. What an exciting turnabout. I was thrilled.

At this time in England it was possible to change careers at twenty-five and work hard to advance in a new career path. The long hours, the hard work, the determination to learn as much as I could from top professionals — writers, producers, camera men — dominated my life. I felt on top of the world. I felt anything was possible. A year later, when I was promoted to trainee news journalist and producer, I cried tears of joy. Finally I was doing something that was intellectually stimulating and worthwhile.

Daily, I worked with my bosses on news stories, often helping to script them, sometimes going out to collect live footage with camera news crews and working in the production department to put together special news programs.

My parents gained social recognition for my efforts. Often on a Sunday night they socialized around the television set, watching a special report, and when my name rolled up on the screen Mum told me Dad's face shone with pride, while Mum said she sat back watching her friends nodding with approval.

During the Gulf War in January 1991, I was at the office from 6:00 A.M. to midnight, the longest and most pressuring hours I ever worked in my life. I was transferred to the editor's office, the helm of the ship, to work as one of his assistants. I was involved in "history in the making"; it was a fascinating period of my life, until one day something happened that burst my euphoric bubble.

# 9

*Age Twenty-Seven, January 1991*

Fifteen men were sitting around the executive editor's table. I had just served coffee and cakes. It was mid-morning and schedules were being discussed, sales options of war coverage to be sold to CNN being evaluated. Twenty television screens down one wall of the editor's room blinked with incoming live footage, electrifying the atmosphere. Suddenly, a red light flashed and then beeped on one of the screens. Everyone stopped talking to watch a scud missile fly a foot over one of our cameramen's heads. Nobody moved; all eyes were fixed on the screen.

There was an explosion. The editor jumped up along with all the men and they whooped and danced around the room. Within a minute they were all cheering each other while the editor was costing the sale of this footage.

This scene unfolded not more than twelve feet from my huge desk with two computer screens and four phones and I just didn't get it anymore. I just couldn't get excited about this groundbreaking moment. I could not relate to the excitement, the meaning of it all in terms of life. I felt dizzy. I felt my throat tighten. I wanted to leave the office and never come back. While I knew something important was happening that was good for the company, I suddenly disconnected; what we were doing and what it meant to me suddenly lost all meaning. Who was I? What was I doing here?

"Pop" went this career balloon.

Two months later, after the company's expenditure had sky-rocketed during the war, I was let go from my job. I was relieved. Dad, for the first time, was verbally compassionate and equally devastated.

Now I had no choice. I was a free bird with no excuses. I had to do what I should have done earlier in my life; it was time to seek the truth and turn over every stone to find the most suitable way to live in the most suitable place in the world.

# 10

*Uttar Pradesh, India, late summer 1992*

I am standing by a wriggling piece of dirty rag on a rug where a family — father, mother and ten mostly little children — are sleeping in a puzzle-piece order, surrounded by their worldly possessions — pots, basic food supplies, toothbrushes, piles of clothing and sandals.

I scan the faintly lamp-lit street carpeted with souls all sleeping in a similar abode and then look back at the now open piece of fabric. I see a baby girl, perhaps a day or two old. Her brown eyes shine brightly; her little hand reaches up to the sky as she tries to find her balance. I kneel beside her and look into her eyes. She is perfect, but her life seems totally imperfect and inappropriate for a child of G-d. I want to gather her up and take her back to London, to give her a home and a life that would surely be far better than this; a place on a carpet in a street of people under the sky.

At this moment, I recognize this Indian baby's destiny and I become aware of my own, that of a Jewish girl far from anything familiar in this country so far from home. The dichotomy is awesome, vast, beyond me. There is a world of difference between our lives, our legacies, our futures — or is there?

At this moment, I want to be out of India, far away. India, this country, this way of life, this family are the little baby's — they don't belong to me. What am I doing here so far from what is mine? I am a Jewish girl, not an Indian girl; but what difference is that making to my life? Why did I travel to India in the first place? For a split second I'm not sure anymore.

I make a promise to myself to look into Judaism more seriously when I return to England but within a day this pledge is relegated to the back of my mind. Passing through a mesmerizing country for six weeks, I get swept up in a captivating adventure.

India was after America, France, Italy, Switzerland, Germany, Austria, Hungary, Spain, Portugal, Greece, Turkey, Egypt, Israel, Hong Kong, China and Thailand. Twelve years of traveling, of looking, of stepping into other people's worlds. I had exhausted myself, physically, emotionally, intellectually and spiritually in search of something that felt right, true, perfect for me.

I returned to London in September 1992, depleted and despairing; years of earning a living, of listening to others, of observing, reading, questioning, discussing and wandering had not brought me closer to a life of purpose or contentment or a life devoid of loneliness. I was still single and searching. I was still lost.

I was also twenty-eight years old and becoming aware for the first time of a major issue that was blocking my development; I hadn't thought about marriage or having children and that was finally bothering me. No one had broached the subject with me or painted this picture for me and I cannot say that I yearned for it with all my heart. Yet, it seemed the inevitable next stage, according to the social norms. I knew I was disconnected from the idea and the preparation for it. My parents had assumed I would marry the first boy I dated — some ten years back — and when I didn't because I didn't feel ready for such a big commitment, I feel they gave up hope in me. Since then social relationships had always taken a back seat to career advancement.

Now back from India, I was once again in a perplexed state. I spent the week following my return scribbling concerns in a journal and fasting during the daylight hours for mental and emotional clarity. All this transpired while I tried to hold onto my current contract at PolyGram as a marketing assistant in an international record company, a place which was far from the ideals of simplistic, spiritual living which I had just encountered in India and a job that was not proving to be as satisfying as I hoped.

On the evening of the sixth day of my fast, I retired in a hopeless state. Where would my salvation come from? How was I going to change my life for the better? Was I destined to work at jobs that lost their appeal every few years for the rest of my life? Would I be single forever? What was wrong with me? The girls and boys I had met at Jewish clubs and the majority I had met socially in my teens and early twenties or through my work appeared to have a life of value. Many of them owned property, they ran up-and-coming successful companies, they were getting married, some were married and starting families. All of these people seemed to be content with London life and their lot. Perhaps I was looking for a place to live and a lifestyle with a person who didn't exist. What was to become of me? What would be my story? I felt miserable. I felt like a failure. I felt incompetent and directionless; the feeling was awful. And I didn't know whom to speak to about the mess I was in.

I worried about my priorities and outlook on life. Jewish girls marry "nice Jewish boys": accountants, lawyers, doctors, jewelers, property agents, businessmen or stockbrokers like their fathers or brothers. Why hadn't this happened to me? Why didn't this interest me? Marriage just wasn't on my "to do" list. I was okay with this until I returned from India; now I realized my way of thinking wasn't normal.

For now, as the sixth day of my fast came to an end, I was being soothed by piano music drifting in through the window of my new rental apartment around the corner from my "Penguin editor" friend. The beautiful music was lulling me to sleep, as a new moon hung in the black sky and I prayed for a solution to my predicament.

# 11

At 7:45 A.M. I hurried out of my apartment and literally bumped into a young woman coming out of the adjacent door from the upstairs apartment.

"Oh, I'm sorry, are you okay?" I said to the petite, dark-haired stranger.

"Yes, I'm alright. Thanks," she said in a New York dialect. She held out her hand. "My name's Susie. I arrived yesterday. Did you hear me playing last night?"

"That was you? Yes, it was wonderful; I love piano music," I said.

"I'm here on sabbatical with the Philharmonic Orchestra," she said.

We chatted for a few minutes; Susie was easygoing, a friendly trusting soul, unlike anyone I had met before.

"What are you doing tonight? Want to come to a talk by this rabbi on the next block?"

I laughed. What was she talking about? I had lived in Little Venice, Maida Vale in central London for nearly three years and I'd never seen any rabbis in the local vicinity that looked anything like the "Orthodox-affiliated" rabbis in Raleigh Close Shul in Hendon.

That night I went to the home of Rabbi Rashi Simon and his wife Ruthie, an Orthodox Jewish American couple, who had established a Jewish learning program in their home. No wonder I hadn't noticed Rabbi Simon; he was clean-shaven and neatly dressed in a tailored suit, just like any other well-groomed businessman. In the lecture, I was part of a group of around fifteen men and women in their twenties. After a thought-provoking two hours of a most fascinating talk and lively discussion where questions were welcomed, even encouraged, I returned home inspired and reflective. I had just met a warm, welcoming family who were offering a university-like learning experience a street away from my home. Here I could learn new ideas and have my mind challenged; what an amazing opportunity. I was intrigued and decided to return later in the week.

From these inconspicuous beginnings I popped over to the Simons most nights for scheduled lectures, mostly on different aspects of Jewish thought, or a chat with Rabbi Simon. The Simon's open-door policy made it comfortable to drop in anytime, which was pretty unusual by English standards.

Both husband and wife were gracious, educated and inspiring and they accepted me for who I was; they didn't reprove me for my inquisitiveness, they didn't judge me for my probing questions or new feelings. Within a few months I was a regular Shabbos guest and every one of my questions was welcomed with an enthusiastic reply and explanation. The Simons' extensive lending library was thrown open to me. Rabbi Simon oversaw my reading list, pacing my gathering of knowledge about authentic Judaism so I wouldn't overdo it. Spiritually starving, I was eager to learn everything but listened to my new "coach" who guided me thoughtfully.

Soon after my first few *Shabbosim*, Rabbi Simon introduced me to Rabbi Yisroel and Julie Roll, a Canadian and American, who had moved to London to be the Rav and Rebbetzin of the New West End Synagogue, Notting Hill Gate shul near Hyde Park. The Rolls invited me to their nightly lectures and for Shabbos lunches.

Very soon, the Simons and the Rolls became mentors, close friends, people I chose to spend time with and emulate in my own way; they lived a way of life that attracted me, intrigued me, enthused me. I believe experiencing a Torah-true Shabbos was the turning point in my decision to pursue a more in-depth study of Judaism and embrace that choice with a sense of bewildered joy.

I had never felt this way before; I had never wanted to take ownership of anything in an encompassing manner until I experienced Shabbos. Shabbos was a wonderful new discovery that took time to grasp and put into practice. Slowly but surely, the luxury of time and space the twenty-six hours of Shabbos gave me allowed me to ponder and then reassess my lifestyle, value system and decision-making process. Shabbos transformed a regular Saturday into an oasis of peacefulness and thoughtfulness a world apart from the other six days of hectic, dynamic living.

At the outset, Shabbos was a challenge. It curbed my flighty personality, it was initially uncomfortable to exchange my secular habits for a peaceful day around the home and my vicinity devoted to prayer, family life and a Jewish ideal. When I met the Simons I was freelancing with different companies to fund exploratory trips to foreign lands. I was a free agent who did what I wanted when I wanted. Sometimes Shabbos was difficult; I was challenged to exchange a lifetime of secular habits for a new way of living by a set of laws that were not mandated by regular society, my parents or myself — for one day. Shabbos became a window into a whole new world, a whole new way of living and being that was in essence Jewish. Each week, as I adhered more closely to more Shabbos laws and got more inspired by the spirit of the day an unusual thing happened; secular influences and temptations fell along the wayside and other more worthwhile experiences entered my life.

My commitment to Shabbos was my first commitment to me; I

dedicated a period of time to something that was truly mine — my Jewish legacy.

After years of wandering I didn't have to leave London to go to some far-flung place in the world in search of that elusive something that I now had taken possession of. I was learning to appreciate my own faith and how to live it — at home — the most perfect place to start visualizing my new hope for the future of being a wife and homemaker when I was ready to make this commitment to marriage. My new role models were showing me, by example, what I now only dreamed might be possible for myself one day — when I was ready.

When I was ready? Surely this is an odd remark; at twenty-eight-years old surely I was old enough to do what I liked, go where I wanted, be who I wanted to be, and marry whom I liked.

That is absolutely true, but the life I had lived so far and the person I was at that time was not freeing me to do what was right for me. I felt enslaved to my life and my alter-ego; at twenty-eight I felt worthless and lost in the scheme of the secular world.

When I entered into the Orthodox Jewish world of the Simons and the Rolls, I met four people who were one hundred percent committed to an authentic way of living that originated from a way of life that was part of who I was intrinsically as a person. These relationships made an indelible impact on me and prompted me to make a choice, to take a journey that I prayed would lead me in a new direction. I made this choice consciously and was agreeable step-by-step, day-by-day, mitzvah-by-mitzvah. (I am still learning the meaning of this statement seventeen years later.)

At this point in my life I was open to change, ready for change, and it appeared to me that G-d had made Himself more visible and willing to guide me on my way.

Undoubtedly, I'd always had promising jobs, wonderful friends, and part of the time I was a self-assured world traveler, but the rest of the time, for reasons beyond comprehension, I was not a content human being — that was the crux of the matter. I had not found a place in the world where I felt at home. I had not met a partner whom I felt comfortable with. Added to this, my life was running ahead at such a fast pace that I was scared that sooner or later I would get lost in the picture of my own life and end up a spinster with a great resume, but not much else.

Shabbos prompted me to slow down and pace my life. When I started to keep elements of Shabbos I had to readjust my life choices. This forced me to come to terms with who I was and with my capabilities. Shabbos at the Simons and the Rolls was the key to seeing marriage in a new light, to experiencing a life of Torah and mitzvos for the first time.

I was ready for change because everything so far — every encounter, experience, and thought — had been transient and had not added to my yearning for a purposeful lifestyle and relationship.

As I brought Shabbos into my life I made room for a Jewish way of life and new prospects which were becoming pleasant and attainable. As time moved on, it didn't make sense to take only Shabbos when there was so much more to own.

Much to my surprise — and this makes me smile every time I think about it — I finally found a guidebook for living that made perfect sense to me when I was twenty-eight years old. Penning these words today gives me much personal joy; I never imagined this would be so after being raised in a Jewish home with Jewish values and Jewish observance, albeit not Torah-based.

# 12

I disliked everything I knew about being Jewish until, when I was twenty-eight, I learned what being Jewish really meant and the potential it held for me.

From as early as my teens I held negative feelings about being a Jewish girl; I recall going to a *Maccabi*, a Jewish social club, with some school friends and thinking I didn't want to be like certain girls who "hang out" there, who only cared about appearances and befriending the "right" boys who drove the "right" cars.

At the public girls school I attended — where us twenty or so Jewish girls were the minority — girls I feared most were a group of particular Jewish girls. They were the class bullies who picked on me because I was different; they didn't like me because I didn't run to join their gang. I kept to myself or spent time with the *intelligentsia* of the class — mostly non-Jewish girls with intellectual and creative interests.

The "bullies" were from lower-class families. They tipped over my desk, scribbled horrible words about me on my school books, punched me in the playground and incited the ring leader to slap my face in the street and spur her pack to hound me during my school years.

By the time I was about thirteen I dreaded going to school. I managed by being an obedient daughter who chose to endure the trial and embarrassment in silence; I was more scared to tell my parents what was happening than to fight the system.

As a youngster I neither read books about Judaism nor got into any sort of discussion about religion and Judaism with anyone.

Watching how Jewish people I liked live their lives, noting how Jewish people treated me: these were my methods for forming an opinion about Judaism.

I had one Jewish friend whom I adored. She was a few years older than me, and we met when I was around thirteen. Her father kept a traditional Shabbos, and over the years I ate at her home often for Saturday lunch after I had been out with my mother in the morning. It was not a Torah home but a very Jewish home. Her father, a kosher butcher, wore a yarmulke when we ate. After the meal my friend and I went for a walk in the park nearby. I loved her parents' warmth and friendship. Her mother kept a neat home, made delicious food, always presented on nice china. They lived simply in a very small, but tasteful apartment in which everything had its place. A feeling of peacefulness and thoughtfulness reigned whenever I was there.

My parents and their friendship circle were proud of their heritage but kept it among themselves. They were traditionalists, members of the local Orthodox synagogue; Mummy lit Shabbos candles Friday night before our meal, we ate matzah on Pesach, went to shul on Yom Kippur and Rosh Hashanah and lit a Chanukah menorah. I did what they did because that was expected; I never knew why or that there was more to these rituals. Our family home had kosher *mezuzos* on the front door, we visited *shivah* houses at appropriate times, and we ate bagels, lox and cream cheese on Sundays for breakfast. I knew I was Jewish but didn't know there was much more to it than the way we lived.

I felt my parents were good giving Jews (and I still feel this way); they were kind and supportive to their Jewish friends, they gave regularly to charities, participated in fundraising banquets for important causes and read *The Jewish Chronicle* to keep abreast of Jewish affairs and to have an opinion on Jewish matters.

My parents introduced my brother and me to Israel for the first time after my brother's bar mitzvah, a grand affair but also the final curtain (for the time being perhaps) on my brother's relationship with Jewish study, but not his connection with a Jewish social set from his English boarding school, who would be his friends for life.

My maternal Bubby and Zeide represented everything that was traditionally Jewish and it seemed old-fashioned and poverty-stricken in my secular materialistic eyes. I adored my "jolly" Zeide, who was born in Warsaw and who ran from Poland to avoid conscription and established a kosher butcher store in Stamford Hill with Bubby, born in England to Russian immigrants. Still, I did

*My Zeide — Avraham Bloom, far left — as a young man.*

not associate their way of life with anything appealing or remotely interesting.

My mother, the spiritualist, referred frequently to her reliance on G-d and pointed to her Bible on her bedside table in the midst of emotional soliloquies. She was an excellent Yiddishe cook; home-baked bread, honey cake, *kneidlach, kreplach,* gefilte fish, you name it, I tasted it throughout my childhood. Although I was intrigued by my mother's references to G-d, which we never talked about, I could never relate to her connection with G-d, as mine had nothing to do with the Bible or an emotional relationship or Jewish cuisine.

While helping my mother in the kitchen, I benefited from an introduction to *kashrus* that Mum had learned from Zeide. I also gained A-to-Z homemaker expertise including cleaning management, efficient systems and guest and entertaining etiquette from helping Mum run the house. My mother also groomed me for public appearances in shul and social gatherings, always making sure I looked right and proper.

Practical hands-on knowledge of loving-kindness was imparted wherever I accompanied my mother; she offered to help people at every turn and regularly stopped at bus stops to offer rides to people in her white, four-seater "mitzvah mobile," as she called it.

Dad, "a regular meat and potatoes man on the dot of seven o'clock," loved Mum's food and her dinner party cuisine. He also liked to eat out; the *heimishe* restaurant Blooms in Golders Green on Sundays — for salt beef, chips and mustard — was a favorite.

My family was Jewish conscious but for reasons that I cannot articulate, even today, I felt more comfortable as a child and teenager with the disassociation.

It's funny: All the years that I was around my parents' friends, who all appeared to be happily married for years, and my parents (who today have been married forty-six years), I never once thought, "I want to be like them and have a life like them." I was hoping my life would be different, even though they all lived privileged lives. I wanted a life with more depth and meaning and was worried sick my whole childhood. Until I met the Simon and the Roll families, I thought what I imagined didn't exist.

The Simons and the Rolls worked for the Jewish community. They didn't talk so much about a lot of things; they simply lived life fully — intellectually, emotionally, physically — with a lively spiritual dimension to their words and deeds. Their lives had essence; they spoke with a sense of deep purpose and they lived with a sense of an awareness of greater ideals with a contagious enthusiasm. They also lived their lives according to a guide book and this is what really interested me the most as I had been looking for such a book for a very long time.

Rabbi Simon loaned me a *Kitzur Shulchan Aruch*, a book that details in summary form the 613 *mitzvos,* the commandments of the Torah. This book, a "how to live life as a Jew step-by-step guide book" flabbergasted me. I knew G-d couldn't have created me and expected me to work out life by myself and I was right.

After reading the *Kitzur Shulchan Aruch* I came to understand that living Torah as a lifestyle, when done in the right way, with the right intentions, gives a person purpose and gratification as well as the potential for great blessing.

About ten years after my conversation with Angelica that Sunday in 1989 I would come to a deeper appreciation of the word *binah yeseirah,* the inner wisdom of a Jewish woman.

*Binah yeseirah* was bestowed by G-d on women; it is an innate knowingness — an intuition — an extra dimension of comprehension about the world and people that women were bequeathed at birth.

Regardless of my youthful ignorance and lack of appreciation about my heritage, and my dislike for all things Jewish until my mid-twenties, I, a simple Jewish girl, possessed innate Jewish wisdom, which I experienced without realizing it until I was able to recognize it for what it was — a gift for life.

# 13

Harold and I are in the park. It is Shabbos afternoon. We have just finished lunch and have offered to look after the Simon children so Rabbi Simon and his wife could take a nap.

The air is chilly, the sky a dull elephant grey; it is a typical English winter day. We are sitting on a bench while the children play on the slides and swings. We are talking about the future. Harold, three years my junior, has been a student of Rabbi Simon's for two years, and I have been learning with the Simons for three months. I am considering a sabbatical for my thirtieth birthday in a year. He has a year remaining of his Master's in holistic medicine.

We talk about marriage, and raising children. Harold talks about what it might be like to live in Israel. I am thinking about my new book publishing job and how, in a year, I will tell them I intend to go to India for a year. A few months earlier I had convinced myself I had just taken my last expedition. Still, I didn't think I would ever shake the urge to run away from the familiar to explore the unknown in the world. I began traveling as a child to tourist resorts with my parents, but by my mid-teens I was traveling to interesting places with friends. My need to leave London, to be in motion, to be free, would never be lost. It was part of who I was. My English name was Vanessa after all, a French name meaning a flock of butterflies. I never wanted to feel trapped like I did in Hendon, like I felt when I was sitting with my paternal grandmother, who had succumbed — so gracefully — to her widowhood and her role as a single mother of two unmarried children, at the age of fifty-four years old. When I traveled, anything was possible; when I traveled I was not tied down or answerable to anything or anyone. I loved that feeling. How could I have that if I were married?

While Harold and I watch the children, I imagine what it might be like to be a mummy. I feel fearful; how will I travel if I have children? Will I have time for my aspirations that have been part of me since childhood?

I voice my concern. Harold thinks by the time I am a mother I won't need to travel. I would have relegated my dreams, that all I will care about is my husband and children, that nothing will matter to me more than to serve their needs and make them happy. The idea sounds entirely utopian; a happy picture for a single Jewish woman. I am not convinced. I cannot imagine it. We exchange more thoughts and give each other blessings for the future.

After we drop the three children back at the Simons' apartment I return home. I sit on my veranda overlooking the internal oval garden of the complex of apartment buildings where I rent my room from Anastasia, an artist in her sixties. She is away for the weekend.

I feel perplexed. Harold's words surface and I push them away; they bother me. Why wasn't I thinking about, desiring, praying for the marriage and family ideal that he was able to express? How can it be that Harold has everything worked out and I don't?

I wasn't honest with Harold; I didn't know him well enough to tell him the truth, that I had been lost for a long time, that I was trying all sorts of things and going to all sorts of places in search of something I hoped existed. I was scared to commit, and to think seriously about the future. I was scared I would take a wrong turn and that I would never find a loving partner. The world Harold saw so clearly in the "heaven" of his mind had captured my imagination, for the first time, three months ago, when I first met the Simons — but could I really get married and have a family? I couldn't imagine it, but maybe now it was possible. If Harold could see it for himself, perhaps I could, too.

I watch the sky darken to indigo blue. I recall an incident that I experienced with Anastasia a few days after my return from India in the late summer, just before I bumped into Susie on my front doorstep and met the Simons.

Anastasia was aware of my "still single" anxieties and my feeling at odds with the world. One Sunday she said, "Why not come to church with me? I have a wonderful time every week. Perhaps you will find what you are looking for there. You certainly haven't found something worth talking about in your own religion." She was right but I was nonchalant until she insisted and I thought, why not?

The church was spacious and attractively designed. Every pew was taken and the air was humming with excitement. The Minister, a large man, fair-colored with blond hair, fair skin and blue eyes, warmly welcomed the congregation before conducting his service. First there was singing, then an easy, attentive atmosphere prevailed during the weekly sermon which focused on extending kindness to strangers.

Halfway through his narrative, the Minister asked everyone to stand and shake the hand of someone we didn't know in the community and smile at them warmly; he wanted us to experience the power of this simple gesture, to feel the effect then and there.

The Minister's suggestion was universal, I didn't find it offensive. In fact, I liked the idea because I felt the world could only become a more manageable, happy place if everyone was a bit kinder to each other.

The moments between the Minister's request and completing the action were passing; my eyes scanned the men and women of all ages and cultures around me and then rested on a man, who had extended his large hand towards me. His face was expectant, his eyes shining, and his smile generous. I looked at him a long while, and then my eyes dropped to the large cross hanging on a chain around his neck. I could not will my hand to take his. I knew at that moment that I was in the wrong place, and suddenly, I had an urgent desire to be small again, small and pretty and sweet in my black patent leather shoes and white socks, and to be standing in the ladies section of our shul in North West London, in Raleigh Close Synagogue, in Hendon, next to my mother and her best friend.

Attending church was just another reminder that I was lost.

# 14

I checked my watch. It was 1:40 P.M.: Richard was due in five minutes. It was only a three minute walk to the Simons where a guest speaker from Israel was going to give a two-hour talk titled "Introduction to *Shidduchim* & Marriage".

I was excited to hear about how religious singles meet their future spouses and conduct their lives in an authentic Jewish marriage. Richard was curious and honest; he was accommodating because he knew I wanted to hear the speaker before we went out for dinner at a new kosher sushi restaurant. We had been friends and then begun dating.

Everything was going quite smoothly in my life. Everything had its "department": the Simons satisfied my intellectual needs, the Rolls provided me with spiritual fare, a new job at a book publisher was physically challenging and inspiring, and Richard was my new oasis of emotional happiness. Now two "departments" would converge: the emotional and the intellectual. I was a little tense about it. What would Richard think about the Simons and what did he really think about all this Jewish "business" that I was becoming more embroiled in?

My parents were very confused about my sudden interest in Jewish studies and my new relationship with rabbis and their wives; my father couldn't quite believe it when I told him I spent Friday nights and Saturdays with two rabbis and their families and that I wasn't at the opera or the theatre or exercising race horses in the country like I used to do. He looked at me quite queerly when

I told him I was enjoying Shabbos and that I couldn't do those things anymore.

I know I must have appeared brainwashed but I had concluded that it was my opinion that really mattered. No one was bending my arm and forcing me into the Simon house on Friday nights. I was choosing to walk in and I did so with much joy and anticipation.

Richard and I found two chairs beside each other near the back of the living room; I was amazed how the Simons had fit one hundred people in their lecture room and that everyone was seated already. The atmosphere was electric; something interesting and unknown to me was about to happen.

The lecturer from Jerusalem, Rabbi Pinchas Schwarcz, was introduced and he proceeded to captivate me; the rabbi spoke enthusiastically and I felt stirred by his words. Richard sat stiffly for the first hour of the talk and in the break took me aside: "I am not ready for this," he said, referring to the fresh news about *shomer negiah* (no physical contact before marriage) and the *shidduch* process (the courting procedure according to Torah Law) and all the other stepping stones to the *chuppah* the Rabbi had touched upon in a modest and sensitive manner.

I looked at Richard, a self-made young man my age. He had kind brown eyes. He had a fine mind and a great passion for life. He was wearing a pale pink Ralph Lauren Polo shirt and casual pants. He was a lovely person; our prospects were good; would I ever find someone else as wonderful? Would I ever have a life as secure as the one I would have with him? Would I find someone as generous and interesting to be with? As I cast my eyes down to tuck in my silk floral shirt that had slipped out of my jeans I kept my eyes lowered a moment longer; I didn't want Richard to see tears that were pressing to fall. I was consumed with sadness. Why did I have to choose now? Why did I have to lose him now? Wasn't there a way to have it all?

I took a deep breath and looked up into Richard's bemused face. I told him that what I was hearing for the first time was something I wanted my children to have and I wanted to own it, too, which meant starting over; doing some sincere *teshuvah*, which I was just learning about and I readily explained as we stood in a corner talking. I said, "I have to learn to forgive myself for my past actions and promise to make certain changes to ensure the future will be different without any repeat actions from the past — to clear the decks for new beginnings and new ways of doing things."

Richard nodded, said he could see the sense in that, but diplomatically excused himself by leaving the Simons' home without sharing his point of view. The risk was great, for a split second I panicked and considered following him out of this new life that was becoming part of me and was claiming me for its own. Then I saw Ruthie Simon in a pretty dress, pass by with a jug of fresh juice and a lovely smile on her face. At that moment she represented the epitome of wifely femininity, modesty and hospitality and I wasn't prepared to give up that vision that I now felt would be best for me for the future.

Could Richard and I have what the Simons and the Rolls had? I doubted it and could feel the tears drop. I fought with the idea that perhaps Richard and I could rewind the clock on our relationship and go back to the beginning. I shook my head; I saw no hope in that idea. For a fleeting second, conflict and despair gripped me. Yet, something powerful inside of me was pulling me back into the lecture room and prompting me to ask questions. I knew I had no control and I was aware for the first time that G-d had finally taken over.

"Come to Jerusalem," Rabbi Schwarcz said, after our private

talk at the Simons' living room table. "You will learn how to live like a true Jewish woman." Rabbi Schwarcz looked at me intently.

I told Rabbi Schwarcz I was thinking of going back to India for my thirtieth birthday in November to meet with the Dalai Lama in Dharamsala. I wanted to discuss my latest reading material on the ethics of Tibetan Buddhism — wisdom, peace and compassion — which seemed to fit in neatly with my emerging Torah-based identity. Even though it was the early days in my investigations, I had not run this new idea by Rabbi Simon.

"Israel's not on the agenda," I replied.

I didn't talk about Richard; I didn't know how to open a dialogue about him with this awe-inspiring holy character from Jerusalem.

Rabbi Schwarcz sat silently still; his calm demeanor quieted my soul. All I could hear was the ticking of the clock in the living room, which was in beat with my sprinting heart.

"Come to Jerusalem as an anthropologist," he shot back so quickly I was taken aback as Richard's image shattered in my mind.

I am still amazed how — in a matter of twelve minutes by the Simons' clock — this Orthodox rabbi, dressed in a long black frock coat, *tzitzis* over his white shirt, white socks, and black hat, who was a former Professor at a well-known American university, now a Torah scholar and international lecturer, had assessed what motivated me and had used the exact word that personified my approach to living. I had been living like an anthropologist; I was an inquisitive person; my fascination and zest for life motivated me to step in and out of other people's worlds, taking away what I pleased.

I saw then how that approach to life was my limitation and one of the causes of my dissatisfaction and disillusionment with life and people. I knew I was afraid of long term commitment. This character weakness was slowly but surely destroying the potential in my life from blossoming in any particular or permanent direction. Even when I was dating Richard, I had doubts about the relationship. So many new aspects of the relationship were good, but was he really interested in me and my mind and the vision I was mulling over for the future? We rarely entered into holistic conversations that touched upon spiritual, emotional, intellectual and material matters. Surely life was a relationship between the four elements, not just a focus on one or two.

The new vision with all its immediate challenges and potential Rabbi Schwarcz presented that winter's day in late January 1993 was something that instantly shocked and intrigued me. His suggestion gave no room for doubt that I had never experienced a culture or lifestyle where I felt comfortable and safe; where I could see myself settling down with someone trustworthy whom I cared about.

I looked at Rabbi Schwarcz. His eyes radiated a sparkle I had never seen before, as well as something I wanted — enthusiasm for a life of purpose. I smiled, then sighed and said, "What a great idea. I've never made the time to investigate my own religion or explore Israel. It's about time. I am a Jew after all."

That afternoon I skipped the one block back to my apartment. Thank G-d Richard, who drove home earlier in his sports car in the break time, hadn't seen me.

Something wonderful had happened that day and I couldn't for the life of me explain it to anyone. I felt energized and cheerful — now I had a plan that made sense — at least to me.

# 15

The next morning I felt meditative while I sat at my desk in the book publishing company, where I worked as an editorial director's assistant. I tried to get through the stack of papers, but I felt heady with the potential that had presented itself less than twenty-four hours ago. I felt remorse about my personal relationship but was hopeful the bigger picture that had presented itself would offer new potential in the future — at the right time.

During lunch break I sat on a bench in the tree-lined square outside the book publisher's West End offices. While the cold January breeze danced around my ankles, I thought about Israel and my first visit to Jerusalem in the heat of the summer when I was fifteen, after my brother's bar mitzvah.

My father hired a driver who drove us around the country on day trips. Our base was the Jerusalem Hilton.

"We're going on a walking tour today," Dad announced to my brother and me over breakfast. We were dressed in T-shirts, shorts and sneakers. The tour guide arrived with a driver and a comfortable air-conditioned car, and we were on our way.

In the Geulah section of Jerusalem, the driver parked his car and the guide started walking while sharing information with anyone who was interested. I was already taking photographs. As a teenager my camera was my friend. Everything looked enchanting and old. My brother held Mum's hand; Dad kept pace with the guide; I straggled behind, clicking away.

We entered Meah Shearim through an archway that had an

overhead sign in Hebrew and English that read: "Dress Modestly." I didn't know what that meant and didn't ask.

The people in Meah Shearim didn't look like anyone I had ever seen before; boys with side-curls and white knitted caps wearing checked shirts and black pants stared at me as I passed. Girls with two long, beribboned braids running down their backs, sporting long-sleeved dresses, turned their heads when I pointed the camera at them. Men and women strode past us, dressed in wintry looking clothes; it seemed odd to me that they wore dark, somber colors on a bright, sunny June day.

The guide led us through a crowded market, down a quiet alleyway, and through an unassuming wooden doorway. We were in a shul.

Mum and I were directed upstairs. The room was narrow. On one side were wood-framed windows that looked down onto the street, where the market stalls displayed fruits and vegetables piled high alongside household goods. The wall on the right was latticed wood with a white lace curtain hung in front of it.

When I looked through the lace and the crisscross of the wood, I saw my father and brother downstairs surrounded by men talking to each other and leaning over heavy books. A singsong hum of foreign words permeated the air. The shul was old, but it felt familiar.

Mum took a few deep breaths and left — I could hear the ricochet of her shoes on the steps. I sat down and picked up a well-thumbed *siddur*. I couldn't read the Hebrew letters, but I held it anyway. With my other hand I touched the lace curtain. It was so delicate, so feminine, and pretty. I looked at my tanned legs, then at my bare tanned arms, and fleetingly felt uncomfortable. I heard someone call my name. For a moment I had forgotten who I was.

Rising from the bench outside the publishing house, I wondered what my trip to Israel would be like this coming summer. A sudden typical London winter downpour was falling fast and heavy. I ran back into the office, dried myself and spent the next hour taking phone calls and typing author notes. The afternoon ticked by while my mind wandered in and out of memories. I thought of my parents on vacation in Israel for my mother's sixtieth birthday.

When the phone rang at three in the afternoon I didn't expect to hear my father's voice — he had never called me at work. "We flew home this morning; your mother is in intensive care at University College Hospital. She has a pancreas infection."

My boss, a towering religious Catholic with a heart of gold, ushered me out the door immediately with words of consolation and encouragement: "Take all the time you need. Call me if I can help in any way."

In a state of sheer panic, I raced along the wet sidewalk without an umbrella. When I arrived by her bedside, I didn't recognize my mother. She wore an oxygen mask. Tubes ran through her nose, and intravenous tubes covered both arms. She looked like a pale, grey, deflated balloon. I was stunned. Although I was familiar with the end-of-life, it was shocking to have it stare me in the face.

I was also grateful: what if Mum and Dad hadn't got back to London and I couldn't get to Israel in time? I knew enough about pancreas infections to know that if they are really bad, they can claim your life in a matter of weeks, if not days. The very idea brought me to tears as I stroked my mother's hand to let her know I had arrived. She was sedated, but I could tell that she knew I was there. A slight tremor of recognition passed across her brow.

The following night I watched the candle flicker for a long time while the moon looked down on me.

"I'll make a deal with you G-d," I said at about 1 A.M. "I'll go to Israel. I'll become *shomeret* Torah and *mitzvos*. I'll get married. I'll make Jerusalem my home, if You give my mother life."

My mother's prognosis was very bad. How many days were left, nobody could say. But what I did know was that my mother was a prizefighter. Perhaps her incredible inner will could help her overcome this terrible situation.

I cried for a very long time after proposing my deal with G-d. I prayed all night for the strength and maturity to honor my word — if, indeed, my mother merited life. At sunrise I was still praying.

Admittedly, I knew very little about my new life of Jewish intellectual interest and Shabbos observance, but what I did know was this was a life of truth and that I was at the beginning of something that appeared to be full of potential.

The next morning at around 9:30 I made my way towards the intensive care unit. I knew I looked awful; I had just seen my reflection and had contemplated going home to sleep and shower before returning later in a better frame of mind, but I knew that I couldn't go home. I had to face the day.

"I don't know what's going on here," said the head doctor, standing outside intensive care. "Your mother made a complete turn-about in the early hours of this morning. I don't understand it. This morning's tests show that something truly extraordinary has occurred. She's going to make it — I do believe she's going to live."

The doctor was surprised by my response — I didn't make one.

Perhaps my prayers had indeed ascended in the night. I could never know this for sure, but one thing was certain: I had made a deal with G-d; He had honored His part of the contract, now I had to honor mine.

G-d had granted my mother a miracle and I was on my way to Jerusalem.

# 16

When my mother's condition stabilized over the next ten days, she was moved to a private room in the rehabilitation unit where they told us she would be for another week. A sense of calm and gratitude prevailed in our family. It was time to request a meeting with my father at my parents' West End apartment. We were sitting in my parents' kitchen when I told him about my plan to study in Jerusalem.

"Aren't you going to India? That's a far better idea for you. Don't you think?" he said.

"No, Dad, that's not the right place for me anymore. I'm going to live in Jerusalem. I want to learn how to be a Torah observant Jewish woman. Then I'm going to get married — and, please G-d, have children."

I placed the brochure about the study center on the counter top. My father peered down, raised his graying eyebrows and gave me a queer look. Thinking back to this conversation, I must have appeared completely absurd and borderline prophetic or, to put it politely, perhaps insane.

"I'm not interested," said Dad, sliding off the barstool, which rocked slightly after his abrupt departure. His half-eaten sandwich sat abandoned on a china plate.

I didn't follow Dad into the living room. I knew, after all these years of our strained father-daughter relationship, that explaining myself would not be advantageous.

*Put your money where you mouth is*, I coached myself, while I took the twenty-five minute walk back to my apartment in Little Venice, Maida Vale.

*Don't be discouraged, honor your side of the bargain,* I thought, as I turned into the home run.

Seven months later, up until a week before my flight, the pressure was on. My parents and some of my friends tried to dissuade me from leaving, but I had my own set of concerns about going to Israel.

An Iranian student at the Jewish Learning Center had had a traumatic experience when he tried settling in Israel; he had gone without his parents' blessing. His father had died a few weeks later. When I heard this story I was greatly disturbed.

"I feel responsible for my father's death," the student told me. "My father said over and over, 'If you go to Israel you will break my heart — and kill me.' They say G-d decides a Jew's arrival and the departure time out of this world, but look what I did — I hastened his departure."

The thirty-something student was inconsolable, even after Rabbi Simon explained it was G-d who called his father back to Heaven; he was not responsible.

"It will take time," said Rabbi Simon.

We, the learning group, also tried to comfort our fellow student. But privately, I wept; I didn't want this to happen to me. My parents were not forthcoming with their blessings. My departure date was approaching and I could see myself canceling my flight at the last moment. I began to feel a sense of impending doom at the thought of being trapped in London for the rest of my life; my vision for the future was fading along with my pledge to G-d.

At a lecture dinner at Rabbi Roll's shul a few weeks later I sat next to the guest speaker's wife.

"You look like you have something on your mind, young lady," she said, after we introduced ourselves. I weighed my options and looked into the mature woman's eyes, deciding on the spot to tell her about my situation and the conflict on my mind.

"I must tell you something important," she said, taking my hands in hers. "In the Ten Commandments, do you know the reason G-d placed 'Remember and Guard Shabbos' above the commandment of 'Honor Your Mother and Father?'"

I didn't know.

"When Jews keep Shabbos, they are saying to the world: We are *shomerei mitzvos*, we honor the Torah. I put G-d — and what He wants from me because He knows me best — above everyone and everything. A Jew is commanded to 'honor' his parents. Did you ever wonder why G-d didn't command us to love our parents?"

I shook my head; I had been listening a lot lately, but had I been asking enough questions?

The speaker's wife continued: "I cannot go into the *halachos* of honoring one's parents now; I recommend you ask Rabbi Roll to teach them to you. But I will tell you this: if one's parents try to dissuade her from keeping Torah, from keeping Shabbos, from marrying a man committed to a Torah way of life, then one must honor one's parents, but not do as they say. Can you imagine how challenging it would be for a Jewish child to keep Torah and *mitzvos* if their love for their parent was compromised because of Torah? I'm sure you love your parents very much, but have in mind you can still love and respect them when you are *shomeret* Torah and *mitzvos*. Don't give up this great gift from G-d for them; you'll regret it the rest of your life. My blessing to you is that you should keep the Torah in Eretz Yisrael like a true Jewish daughter and marry your true *zivug* there."

I looked at this angel from Heaven with complete surprise. I had never heard such a line of thought; it was absolutely astonishing to me.

The speaker's wife tightened her grip on my hands as I tried to hold back the tears. I peered into the eyes of the stranger, who had just given me a great gift of knowledge and the liberty to honor my promise to G-d. Now I felt ready to fly with my hopes while trying to maintain a respectful relationship with my parents. I felt now I could go to Israel with a clear conscience and a peaceful heart.

A few days before my flight, my mother phoned me.

"Please come over tonight. Your father wants to talk to you."

Later that evening I sat in a chair facing my parents. Their body language was formal, their faces ashen. I was anxious but ready for whatever was going to come my way.

"If you think we're giving you the money to go to Israel, I am sorry to disappoint you but we cannot do that," Dad said.

"No, Dad, that won't be necessary. I've paid for my airfare. I also have enough money to last me for about a year."

I didn't dare tell my father that a supportive friend had given me this money as a gift. The silence in my parents' living room was oppressive; the atmosphere miserable. I felt compromised, but I also felt resolved. I never uttered a word to my parents about my pledge with G-d; that was my private business for the time being. Yet, I so much wanted things to be different. I wanted my parents to be thrilled for me. I was on my way to what I felt was a meaningful life for me and my future children who I never wanted to experience what I had felt as a secular Jew; a sense of strain and despair with who I was and how I should live my life. After all, I was choosing to be Jewish in a country that wasn't America, Europe, India or some other foreign place, but a land that was historically connected to my heritage.

Time stood still. I felt my face flush. What would I do if my father said no?

"You have our blessing."

My father's voice was unrecognizable, small and trembling.

I took an intake of breath.

"Write to us and tell us how you are faring," Mum requested, while busying herself with a handkerchief. "You're still my baby wherever you go," she murmured.

I rushed over to hug and kiss her. I tried to smile at my father but I couldn't get my face to honor my desire.

At midnight, seven hours before my mother would come to collect me for the airport, the phone rang in my apartment.

"It's your father here," Dad said. "You've got courage and guts." Then there was a break. "Make sure you write to your mother, so we know how you are managing," he said.

# 17

I am flying through the sky; I am 32,000 feet up in the air. I cannot believe I am on my way to Israel, that I may live there for the rest of my life; the thought is so tremendous, the prospect renders me teary-eyed. Perhaps I am finally growing up, finally learning how to honor my commitments; it feels that way as I think about all my past travels and the feelings of hopelessness and alienation that finally surfaced in India. I pray I will be able to settle my wandering spirit in Israel; that I will learn to travel spiritually rather than physically. I am crying now. The stewardess expresses concern; but I tell her not to worry; something wonderful is happening.

I close my eyes. An image of me sitting in Rabbi Simon's Beginner's Service at the New West End shul a year earlier pops up. I replay the *drashah* that sparked the thought of me finally leaving London to continue my search for that elusive "something" I hadn't found yet.

Shabbos morning *Parshas Lech Lecha* I accompanied Rabbi Simon on the twenty-five minute walk to shul, a new ritual that I appreciated. Rabbi Simon was a generous soul; he let me ask whatever questions were on my mind and answered them in detail. It was a relief to know that no question was irrelevant in his eyes.

I looked at Rabbi Simon as my spiritual mentor. He was helping me make an orderly exchange between Orthodoxy and secularism, inspiring me to tap into my personal potential, teaching me how to take ownership of a new way of thinking, being and living and guiding me through it. His family life was an example of the lifestyle benefits that could be mine. I didn't follow my mentor blindly — I questioned, I debated, I made the choices myself.

Rabbi Simon's weekly Beginner's Service *parshah shiur* at Rabbi Roll's New End Shul was upbeat; I managed to follow his thought processes from the *chumash* and enjoyed the question and answer sessions.

It was fascinating and heartening to hear the other congregants, young single people of all ages, struggling with similar questions and a pleasure to witness their relief when they discovered a gem of an insight.

When Rabbi Simon talked about *Parshas Lech Lecha* and Avraham Avinu's ten tests, my attention was piqued. When he spoke about Avraham Avinu's relationship with Hashem and what Hashem asked him to do ("Go for yourself from your land, from your relatives, and from your father's house to the land I will show you [*Bereishis* 12:1]"), these words affected me profoundly and inspired me to look at my life with a new perspective; I felt they were written for me. I had never heard them before. I concluded if Avraham Avinu had to make such decisions, which on the surface are so counter-intuitive, and he managed and also triumphed, perhaps I could, too.

Now I was on my way to Israel. I thought of Avraham Avinu again and asked myself: Was this my test number one, two, or three?

I let my eyes scan the fluffy-looking clouds outside the window. I let myself cry. It's not easy leaving the city where you grew up, your family, your friends — life as you know it — to walk into the relative unknown, to walk in the opposite direction from everyone else you know and thought represented your world. Would I pass all of the tests that G-d was sure to send my way?

On the journey to Jerusalem I felt an incredible sense of responsibility to my future generations. To calm myself — because the moral obligation seemed so huge — I claimed Avraham Avinu's story and prayed that it would inspire me whenever I needed to push aside whispers of doubt.

Will I regret my choice? What if something goes wrong? How can I possibly return empty-handed to London if I fail? Did I believe enough in G-d to hold on to my hope? Did I believe enough in myself? The questions rolled out and enveloped me but didn't faze me for too long. "Have faith in G-d's plan for you, His Jewish daughter," had been Ruthie Simon's parting words. This mantra calmed me as the plane continued its route to the land I was positive G-d was showing me should be my new home.

PART TWO

# The
# Map Seeker

# 1

*Sunday 15 August 1993: Neve Yerushalayim Campus,*
*Women's Learning Seminary, Har Nof, Jerusalem.*

The taxi driver left me in the car park with all of my worldly
possessions in two suitcases. For five minutes I stood stock-
still, inhaling my decision in the new air with its hint of new
promises. As I looked up into the summer night sky dotted with
thousands of stars, I imagined how amazed and awed Avraham
Avinu must have felt when G-d took him up into the Milky Way
to show him the change of destiny that was due to him now that
he passed his final, tenth test, a destiny that would lead to the
formation of a Jewish nation and the future of Klal Yisrael in the
Land of Israel.

I felt empowered by my choice to come to Jerusalem as I stood
praying I would merit to positively affect the destiny of my future
children under the sparkling skies. The thought was shocking and
exciting all at the same time.

A voice called my name; a girl was walking towards me, her
bright smile and outstretched hand illuminated by the lamplight.
She looked like a beacon on this new planet on Earth. She offered
to carry one of my suitcases and led the way to what would be my
apartment for the next year. Her name was Naomi Kaplan (now
Kramer) and I followed her (and she became my first mentor in
Israel).

That night the house-mother showed me my dorm room — a

roommate was expected in a week — on the second floor of the four-storey building; one of five such buildings in a campus within grass and rose bush gardens. I was a little apprehensive, never having shared a room with anyone. In the meantime, I had to adjust to the new reality of my life: I no longer had an income, I was 2244 miles from my birthplace and I had no idea what my future would be.

I slept soundly in my new surroundings. Bird song drifted in through the window the next morning. Studies were due to start in two days; I spent the intervening time exploring the city.

On my first bus ride out of Har Nof I noticed a familiar-looking man in the aisle across from me. I was so excited; it was Rabbi Pinchas Schwarcz, who had suggested I come to Jerusalem.

Forgetting my sense of decorum, I greeted him and thanked him, while everyone on the bus was looking on in a most surprised manner. Rabbi Schwarcz bowed his head shyly and welcomed me in an unassuming, kindly voice, despite the fact that this was not typical etiquette in Jerusalem's circles. Behaving in a modest manner — the cornerstone of a Jewish woman's conduct — was a lifestyle adjustment, one that I embraced with a great sense of responsibility as time went on.

Rebbetzin Lea Feldman (wife of Ner Yisrael's *rosh yeshivah* in Baltimore) was one of the two counselors at Neve who, in turn, became my advisor; to me she was a personification of modesty. As my role model, she taught me the essence of this trait and the principle of self-awareness and self-forgiveness as I peeled away my past and started to face who I was becoming and who I wanted to be.

*Teshuvah* was a relatively new concept, one that was already becoming a lifesaver while I did a thorough "cleansing" in certain areas of my life. The *teshuvah* process was the key I needed to open the door to my new life in Jerusalem. I had made errors in my past due to genuine ignorance and lack of knowledge of authentic Jewish values; it was a process to come to terms with my past and forgive myself for the choices I had made so I could make the commitment to a Torah way of living. I asked G-d to forgive my past mistakes and help me refine my behavior in line with Torah true values and standards; a lifetime task that I began seriously in the autumn of 1993.

My relationship with Rebbetzin Feldman helped me make a series of initial lifestyle transitions; the discarding of previously held values and the appreciation of new outlooks that slowly but surely felt comfortable and right.

As the months turned into years, Rebbetzin Feldman became my mentor and friend. Eventually she demanded much of me, which I was capable of honoring due to her tutelage and my willingness to go beyond who I thought I was and become who I hoped I could be.

My first few weeks at Neve were attention-grabbing; everybody and everything was new and that kept me absorbed. Morning lessons: *parshah*, Chumash, Jewish Philosophy and the Jewish Way of Life were thought-provoking, but it was the personal time with my new counselor that I looked forward to the most. After my regular attendance at his afternoon lectures, Rabbi Akiva Tatz soon became a spiritual mentor. I followed him around Jerusalem on his lecture circuit.

I had left London euphoric; I was exhilarated at the prospect of new adventures, relationships and possibilities. But after six weeks of Neve classes, I woke up one morning and recognized I was out of the loop of my other life — back in London — and I felt odd, like I had entered a personal wilderness with nothing dynamic to crowd my view, dominate my mind or distract me. With this realization came the enormity of my decision; I was aware of being alone with myself and my choice for the first time and it was a peculiar, curious, new feeling.

Becoming part of the mass of young single female students at Neve was not something I felt completely comfortable with. I was self-consciously older than most of my classmates; I felt more at ease in the company of the married teachers and married women I met through the Simons, the Rolls and my new friend, Naomi, the industrious net-worker.

My choice to spend a year at an all-women's seminary was also quite an extreme choice considering my background. For years I had been ensconced in a social and work network with men and women colleagues and friends. How bizarre it initially felt to be in a woman-only environment modeled on a college infrastructure with Torah ideals as the educational foundation. One of my ongoing challenges was to explain myself to my parents and brother. Eventually, I forewent explanations and simply got on with constructing a new life without talking too much about it.

# 2

In late summer, the Jerusalem days are long. Very early Friday morning I take an Egged bus to Ashdod. Ten minutes from the bus station is the beach, the place where I feel a need to air my thoughts.

The breeze is warm already, the sky a brilliant cloudless blue, the sound of quiet a balm for my soul.

I walk out to the ocean's edge. I watch the tide roll in and out. I let my eyes rest on the beautiful colors and take long deep breaths. Then I open a dialogue with G-d, for it is for Him that I came all this way; this is the place I feel Him most right now. Neve is noisy, Jerusalem is hectic; I need space and silence to think.

I am alone. I am far from everything, just as I wanted. London is thousands of miles away; so is everything familiar to me. Now what? G-d, what now?

I look out over the ocean; the day is opening. New potential is about to be born. I let my eyes scan the horizon, search beyond what I can see into the map of my dreams.

What next?

G-d, what next? Tell me what to do, where to go, how to be. I am here listening. Don't abandon me! I need you. I am here listening for the answers like I have always been. Since I was a child. When I was a teenager. And now in the Land of Israel, my new home.

Show me the new map.

Show me which new path to take.

Just an edge.

Just a clue.

Just help me to continue believing in me, the plan, the possibilities, in You.

Help me to continue being a dreamer. Help me arrive one day. Help me to succeed on this journey in this lifetime.

The peacefulness frightens me. I hear nothing but my breathing and the waves ebbing and flowing. The sound of silence unnerves me. I sit down. I rest my head on my knees and cry.

# 3

At Neve restlessness consumed me sooner than I thought. Being confined to a classroom wasn't something I was used to or relished doing for the next year. Sitting in a library all afternoon with a tutor also became wearisome as my eyes wandered beyond the page, out the open window where they scanned the azure cloudless sky and the forested valley that disappeared over rolling hills into the far distance.

The view was inviting; I yearned to be free, like the birds soaring through the sky and to be on the move meeting new people and seeing new places, which was the part of my nature I was denying. My bi-monthly visits to the beach to walk and talk to G-d where sustaining but I wanted more space to think, to see the future more clearly.

Naomi hit upon a solution; during the Sukkos break, I accepted a *chessed* opportunity in the North of Israel, in the city of Tzfas.

How wonderful it felt to be in motion again and how beautiful was the land I passed through on the four-hour bus ride; the Jordan mountain range tinted purple and brown filled one side of the vista for miles. The groves of fruit orchards ran for long stretches; to meander languidly and inhale the heady fragrance would be something I would like to do — one day.

Perched on a mountain, Tzfas appeared as we took a bend on a steep ascending road. The address Naomi had handed me was a two-storey building facing the green Meron Valley, the resting place of the holy man Rabbi Shimon Bar Yochai, the foremost student of Rabbi Akiva, who adopted the way of Torah when he was forty years old and went on to be a great Torah scholar and leader.

I contemplated Rabbi Akiva's story as I took in the vast magnificent view that skipped on for miles and miles; I was twenty-nine turning thirty in a month and feeling like life had begun all over again thirteen months ago, when I discovered authentic Judaism. What would my destiny be now that I had taken a new pathway? I inhaled the fresh mountain air while plucking up the courage to meet my host family.

The worn wooden door was opened by a man who introduced himself as Rabbi Aharon Berger. Small children were pulling at his long black frock coat, and a few older ones stood to his side. "My wife had to remain in the hospital with the new baby. She'll be back in about a week," he said.

Naomi's telegram-like note — "Tzfas family needs help urgently" — lacked a few details. I looked into the kindly face of this stranger with a beard and shining eyes and then I looked into the kitchen and saw some more children who had turned their heads towards me. I must have appeared surprised. Rabbi Berger said, "The way I see it, you have two choices: hop on the next bus back to Jerusalem or stay." He then smiled, as did the children.

I had wanted an adventure and that is exactly what I got: for the next week I experienced what it felt like to manage a home with seven children aged two to twelve which brought out the best and most creative in me, much to my surprise and amusement. I enjoyed the tasks at hand, even — and this one makes me laugh the most — attacking a laundry mountain that had amassed over the past week. I was pleased when my simple yet innovative strategy to bathe four reluctant girls Erev Shabbos was successful. I sprinkled rose petals on the water and asked who wanted to smell like a Shabbos rose *l'kavod* Shabbos *kodesh,* which worked like a dream.

The father of the family, a *rosh yeshivah* and a patient soul, showed me, practically — not from a book — how to infuse *avodas* Hashem with spontaneous joy. His ability to break into song and dance and to tell enchanting and funny stories at any time of day helped defuse family challenges, which made for an easygoing home atmosphere.

I used the Rosh Yeshivah's approach to tap into my own potential and creativity. I came up with new ways to deal with all sorts of challenges. Daily, my satisfaction increased while my fondness towards an authentic Jewish family life grew.

In Tzfas I experienced for the first time what was to become beloved to me — Sukkos. We ate our meals in the sukkah under the palm leaves and I listened to the children and guests singing *zemiros* and I realized how fortunate I was to be in Eretz Yisrael having this incredible experience.

Many times while I was in the Berger home, I forgot a Torah way of life was new to me; no one made me feel inadequate and I certainly didn't feel that way. I felt like I really belonged; there were moments when I was in the midst of a task that I felt like I had lived this way always and it was delightful.

I got teary-eyed when I accompanied the smaller children to shul Erev Yom Tov, as images where I saw myself in the future experiencing this with my own family appeared to me, and it was the most beautiful feeling I have ever known.

*The real thing — my own future family — can only be better*, I wrote in my journal. *I am getting a feeling of what it must be like to be a mummy and it is lovely.* I scribbled to G-d because now my journal notes were addressed to Him in a sort of prayer-like way. It was worth coming to Tzfas for this.

My relaxed state and smile were proof of my happiness as I tried to push aside the fact that this wonderful thing called "family life" would soon end for me when I returned to Jerusalem. Any doubts or fears I may have had about committing myself to living a Torah life faded in Tzfas. The experience was giving me a taste of something I was convinced I could live in its entirety with the help of G-d, and of course, a husband.

I do not know how I managed to fit it in during the two weeks I ended up staying at the Berger home — because looking after the family was nearly a full-time job — but while I was in Tzfas, I also experienced my first encounter with a *shidduch* under the careful guidance of the Rosh Yeshivah.

I thought I knew everything about dating before I met Meir, a newly religious young man, who was a year ahead of me in his commitment to authentic Judaism. Very early on in the proceedings, I realized I knew nothing about *shidduchim*: the Orthodox Jewish way to date and the stepping stones to engagement, the *chuppah* and a Torah-true marriage.

When the Rosh Yeshivah made the unexpected suggestion that I go out with Meir, I was enthusiastic; the family experience in the Berger home had enthused me about the idea of being a wife and mother. However, I was about to learn a mature commitment to a Torah way of life and an appreciation of what that really entails are prerequisites for Orthodox marriage.

# 4

The day Meir and I had our first date, I began to grow up — rapidly. Going on a *shidduch* was radically different from anything I had experienced. Mostly we went for walks in public places, spending limited time together, where we spoke openly and directly about our dreams, hopes and needs for the future. I preferred it to secular dating because there was a purpose to our encounter; we were meeting to see if we were suitable for each other for life. But as each day passed with a new date, I realized I was in over my head; I was too inexperienced to handle the responsibility. How could I possibly be thinking of marriage when I was so new to this way of life?

After expressing my concerns to the Rosh Yeshivah, he encouraged me to share my feelings with Meir, which I did with trepidation. Meir felt the same way; we slowed everything down. With the pressure off, we were more at ease to reveal our true selves; this lightness made the dating much more pleasant, but somehow more intense. Eventually, we couldn't see the way forward. I was sad but also relieved as images of my past relationships jostled my mind and I realized I had so far to go and so much *teshuvah* to do before I would be ready to date anyone again with a clear mind and heart.

Back at Neve Yerushalayim, concentration eluded me. My studies and my sleep suffered. I had entered *shidduchim* too early; the experience had disturbed my peace of mind. Finally, I shared my dilemma with the Simons in London. Rebbetzin Ruthie faxed helpful guidelines:

"Carry on learning and integrating. Go to your highest level; reach your truest personal potential as a religious woman and then your true essence will reveal itself. At this stage, you will be ready for *shidduchim* and marriage. In marriage you will move through new and more enriching stages with your partner, but you have to be more developed and aware of what would be appropriate for yourself before making this lifetime commitment."

When I read this fax I felt relieved and humbled. I certainly was not ready to make a lifetime commitment. The Simons knew me best. Why hadn't I turned to them about something so fundamentally important earlier on in the *shidduch* process?

It was a tough lesson; an unhealthy part of my ego was still controlling my life. When was I going to realize that Torah is truth? When would I internalize that what *Chazal* teach is right: two heads are better than one. Talking about things with those more knowledgeable was the only way for me to progress and grow in a healthy way.

# 5

It was a challenge to return to Jerusalem; I liked acting the part of mummy and homemaker. It gave me a sense of real-life purpose.

Back in my dorm room, I was ordinary me and it felt inappropriate considering my age and aspirations. I knew I was a doer, a giver, and I now knew I wanted my own family, but I knew I'd have to temper this need to be active while I attended classes. I was frustrated and concerned about the future and how long it would take for me to actualize dreams that were part and parcel of becoming *shomeret* Torah and *mitzvos*. I had a problem sliding back into the Neve routine. I shared my woes with Chanie, my nineteen-year-old roommate. With Chanukah on the way, she suggested we see a rabbi for a *brachah* and advice.

I recall what I wore the day I met Harav Chaim Pinchas Scheinberg *shlit"a*; the Rosh Yeshivah of Torah Ore and a rav who makes himself available to his *talmidim,* his Mattersdorf community, and every Jew who comes to his home in the afternoon. As Chanie and I waited in the foyer for our turn, I reviewed what I wanted to say. It was a cold, damp winter's day, and I was dressed from head to toe in navy blue.

When I was ushered into the living room I hesitated at the door as I took in the magnitude of what came into vision; sitting behind a table piled high with *seforim* was a small-faced man, perhaps in his early eighties, with a pale shiny forehead framed in white hair. He was wearing *tefillin* and what appeared to be a thick layer of cream *tzitzis* over a white shirt, which was, in fact, a large quantity of perhaps fifty or more *tzitzis* by the width of the compressed fabric rather than the usual one pair of *tzitzis* worn by religious men. The vision was unusual; a petite, radiant man ensconced in a huge mountain of white. An aura of calm radiated from Rabbi Chaim Pinchas Scheinberg; all I could sense was pureness, wisdom and acceptance. It was an unfamiliar realization but one that made me feel safe and unruffled in the company of an auspicious stranger.

The darkness of my attire contrasted with the Rav's lightness and I immediately realized I had far to go before I would be able to transcend the darkness within myself.

Concerned about what one says to such a personage, I had asked my spiritual mentor Rabbi Akiva Tatz for advice. "The words will come. You'll know what to say," he'd answered.

He was right. After speaking, I waited for the Rav's advice, but the Rav simply said, "Amen."

I remained silent, thinking there would be more. Rebbetzin Bessie Scheinberg, the Rav's wife and equal in age, came to my aid; my request for an explanation wouldn't surface; I was star-struck.

"The Rav said 'amen' to your words; making your words the *brachah*," she said. "He is blessing your words so they should be answered."

I was momentarily speechless and then felt incredibly emotional and expressed my gratitude for the Rav's kindness; how giving a gesture and how magnificent the word "amen" can be.

I looked at the Rav, who was sitting on a throne-like chair with wide armrests where his white-sleeved slim arms lay, his wrist dressed in a gold watch.

"Stay a while and get to know the Rebbetzin and her sister Rebbetzin Shain and my daughter Rebbetzin Altusky," he said, raising his hand in a sort of welcome gesture. "My wife will prepare for you a cup of apple juice. The women are in the kitchen."

He then smiled and laughed.

I liked Harav Chaim Pinchas Scheinberg. I turned to smile at his wife, I liked her also; both husband and wife were kind and welcoming and that felt so good on a cold, damp, winter day.

# 6

December in Jerusalem heralded a shift in season; since August the sky had been consistently blue, the air warm or hot, and the breeze minimal.

With the arrival of winter, the weather was unpredictable. Some days I thought I was back in rainy, grey England, other days I enjoyed January or February wearing a cotton shirt and humming with pleasure from the cloudless blue above and the early blossoming roses below in the gardens outside my campus dorm window.

In early April, when the weather had evened out to a common denominator reminiscent of the endless blue ribbon of summer, a phone call came in our dorm building late one evening; a woman casually asked if anyone wanted to help a couple of women cook for Pesach. I thought that sounded like a fun idea and agreed.

The following afternoon I met the women who needed help; two *Chassidishe* rebbetzins — Raichel Horowitz, the wife of the Grand Rabbi Levi Yitzchak, the Bostoner Rebbe *shlit"a* and his daughter-in-law, Rebbetzin Sima Horowitz. They were sitting in the Pesach kitchen in the basement of Rebbetzin Sima's house in Har Nof beside plastic-covered tables laden with raw food. Light streamed into the room from a long wall-to-ceiling window running along the full length of the room overlooking a treed small garden. Huge sacks of vegetables were scattered on the floor and a long list of scribbled notes were visible from where I stood.

"Before we begin working," the younger rebbetzin said, "I want to thank you for agreeing to help us and to explain something; it's our *minhag* to prepare all our own food for Pesach. We have a lot to do. You can start with peeling those," she said, pointing at a knee-high sack of potatoes.

I didn't feel like peeling so many potatoes but I heard a voice inside of me say: give this a chance, be obliging, you are going to learn so much. These are women the likes of which you have never met before. How can you not gain something special from the time you will spend here?

Over the next two weeks I helped at the Horowitz house every evening. While the three of us worked side by side preparing the food and listening to the *alter* rebbetzin's woven tapestry of Old Country stories, I experienced many uplifting moments.

Both women chatted comfortably like mother and daughter as they worked side by side, often drawing me into the conversation by asking questions about who I was and where I had come from. At times they referred to the potential for personal growth at this time of year, a new idea to me. My recollections of Pesach at home in Hendon only existed of struggles, domestic frenzy, digesting unpalatable matzah and drinking four cups of wine that left me feeling heavy-headed.

As Pesach neared, listening to new teachings and new ways of viewing life made me realize — once again — the limitations of my understanding of authentic Jewish life. Expectations mounted when the rebbetzins extended an invitation to me to be a guest at the Grand Rabbi, the Bostoner Rebbe *shlit"a*'s Pesach Seder and they insisted I eat my Chol Hamo'ed meals with their family.

In my spare time leading up to Pesach I reviewed my lesson notes from Neve; pondering on the possibility that every Jewess can find herself in the story of Pesach.

As this historical spiral of time was returning I learned about the importance and value of re-telling the story of the Jewish people's emancipation from slavery; the re-telling often inspires a person to re-write their own story of personal liberation from a slavery that they or others impose. A narrowness of thinking, speaking and behavior can be a form of slavery that limits growth and potential to serve G-d.

Eretz Yisrael was now my home; by some miracle I had freed myself from the limitations of my London life. I was now ready to open myself up for unlimited opportunities in Jerusalem. I was heady with the thought of the potential of my future.

Erev Pesach I helped the *alter* rebbetzin and her son Rav Mayer Horowitz *shlit"a*, prepare the table for the sixty or so guests. Two hours later the table was set with fine china, silver flatware place settings, silver artifacts, crystal glassware and fresh flowers; the ambiance reminiscent of a royal household.

The night felt like a regal occasion and was like nothing I had ever experienced. The telling of the Haggadah — repeated by the guests — was led by the rebbe and, in places, sung by the men and boys.

Three A.M. heralded the arrival of about thirty of the rebbe's chassidim. Dressed in white knee-length *kittels*, crowned in fur *shtreimels*, they had the appearance of an assembly of angels. Near the close of the Haggadah, the rebbe led his court of chassidim in a melodious Hallel (which was my first, and I have replayed it in my mind hundreds of times because it was the most magnificent visual and audio experience), and then the first night of the holiday concluded with me floating home just before dawn.

The evening was out of this world; this was what it meant to have Pesach as a Jew? I never knew this option existed; I was amazed.

When I entered my dorm room at Neve Yerushalayim, a tinge of sadness accompanied a question that hounded me while I sat on the edge of my bed in a sort of mystical daze: why had I come to this lifestyle so late in life? Instantly I corrected myself; this gift was what G-d was giving me now. *Take it*, I thought *and be very, very grateful.*

# 7

As the end of my year on Neve's campus approached, I panicked. Yes, the year had been productive; every day was ripe with opportunity. The learning had been enlightening and life-changing. The tours around Israel with my fellow students had deepened my love of the Land of Israel. My new relationships and all the memorable experiences I had been granted were re-shaping my outlook on Judaism — but by June 1994 I had run out of money.

I made an appointment to speak to the campus dean.

"I don't have any money left," I simply said.

The dean acknowledged this fact with a slight nod, but didn't respond.

"I'm leaving Neve in July. I'm not going back to London. This week I'm interviewing for a job as a counselor at a Jewish learning program. I get free board and lodging. It will mean moving to the Jewish Quarter in the Old City," I said.

"Why?" he asked, from behind his wide desk.

"I need to earn some money. I have made a plan; everything will work out."

"Hashem will give you what you need. You don't need to leave Neve — yet. Another year would be best for you," he said.

"I'm very worried. How will I stay in Israel without money? I want to stay in Israel."

"Hashem will provide," he said, without adding how.

I looked at the English rabbi, whose reputation for wisdom and frugality preceded him. Perhaps he didn't understand me; I was penniless and seized with the need to remain in a country that had become beloved to me. The only way to do this was to go back to work to pay my way.

I knew there was a G-d; I had been "feeling" Him and "seeing" Him in all sorts of ways since I was a little girl. But perhaps I didn't "know" Him that well or trust in Him enough — yet. This must have been so because I still held on to the belief that "I" was in complete control of my destiny and "I" knew all the answers.

I was headstrong. I didn't open a dialogue with the dean; I just stated my intentions. He tried to tell me something important, but I couldn't "hear" what he was trying to tell me. All I knew was what I "felt" and could "see"; I needed to stay in Jerusalem and I had no money. It was as simple as that for me, so I left Har Nof.

# 8

I moved into Jerusalem's Old City in the summer of 1994. The next twelve months took me on a new road; it was equally different from the *Chassidishe* world of the Bostoner Rebbe *shlit"a*'s court, and from the *Litvishe Chareidi* community in Har Nof.

My job was as a counselor on a Jewish learning program for Ivy League students; intellectuals studying Torah and Jewish Thought for the first time in Jerusalem. Their probing questions ignited a sort of passion in the group, which made for an invigorating ten weeks.

All the participants moved at lightening speed in their appreciation and understanding of the authentic Jewish way of life. A handful of the boys stayed on to learn in a yeshivah, and the same amount of girls went to seminary. Many returned home with a commitment to live a more Jewish-conscious life.

After this program I joined another, this time with sixty recent graduates from Australia.

And so, a new bright bunch of excited young people descended on the Old City for a program that included extensive travel around Israel.

Spring was in the air and Israel looked stunning as we explored the country. I enjoyed this program very much. The variety, content and pace had a positive effect on everyone. My favorite experience was a two-day stay-over on our way to Mount Hermon in the Golan Heights. The first day we had bobbed down the Jordan River fully clothed wearing sun hats sitting in oversized tires and had good old-fashioned wholesome fun — something I hadn't done for a while. It felt so good to laugh again; I had been caught up in a serious mood for too long worrying about earning a living and what would be with my future prospects in Jerusalem. Relaxing in a modest way was a great tonic.

Later that day we had a barbeque around an open fire while the boys sang Jewish songs. There was a wonderful atmosphere amongst the group of *achdus* and camaraderie.

Another day we made our way through lush, green pastures under blue skies to the snowy mountain range of Mount Hermon at the tip of Israel.

Israel is a fascinating country full of contrasts and surprises; all the weathers of the seasons and all the landscapes of the world can be found in this unique little space on any one day. While we enjoyed our exhilarating day of tobogganing in the north, visitors in the hot weather in the south of Israel were scuba diving in the coral reefs in Eilat.

This program enhanced my love of my country and my faith. I fell in love with Israel and my choice to stay and become *shom-eret* Torah and *mitzvos* all over again; the curriculum of the last program I worked on was rooted in authentic Judaism, the issues debated were contemporary and intriguing. I felt elated at the close of the six weeks and thrilled when I was offered a public relations position to promote similar programs. The position had personal meaning; the Jewish connection made me feel honored to be doing something exciting and supportive for Klal Yisrael.

# 9

The Old City of Jerusalem's Jewish Quarter had a welcoming women's community; I made new friends easily and enjoyed the local *shiurim*.

Walking through the charming cobble-stoned maze of narrow streets, made up of holy sites and residential homes, I entered the inner world of the Jewish Quarter, which never failed to enchant me. The area, mostly blocked off to outside traffic, permeated *kedushah*. Living in the Old City was like living history, the old and the new merging day-in and day-out.

I didn't miss London's hectic and noisy environment that clogged my mind with mounting car fumes and intrusive advertising; the modern world's "anything goes" value system has a habit of overtaking one's mind if your diligent watchdog isn't on guard.

To the dismay of my family and friends, I was now living in what they described as a ghetto-like existence or "an ostrich with his head in the sand" mentality.

These descriptions didn't upset me; there was a touch of truth in their interpretation but how else was my emerging Jewish soul to be protected from inappropriate, detrimental secular influences?

Secular London life eventually took the guise of a wild jungle, with unknown forces lurking in dark corners that turned out to be misleading and dangerous for all aspects of my being. Surely my way of life in Israel and being *shomeret* Torah and *mitzvos* would ultimately honor and protect my soul and my choices and help me prepare for a happier and safer future, not only for me but for my children.

At this point, I realized one of the highest barriers to transcend is the one that separates you from other people's misplaced priorities; if you make a successful leap, the excitement and trepidation you feel when you land in an unfamiliar appropriate territory justifies the separation anxiety you experience and the strength and stamina you need to get there.

My head wasn't in the sand; my eyes were wide open. I knew what I was doing. I knew where I was going and why I had made the choices I was still making. My life was anything but boring or narrow minded; in fact, I had never felt more excited about my life.

After two years in Israel I had decided a Torah life was a privilege. I believed the way I was living was a gift from G-d. I felt my existence was not contingent on waiting to receive direction from G-d; it was contingent on using my free will and aligning my free choice with what G-d thought was best for me. I felt my *tafkid* was to use my intelligence to live my best life in my own unique way, using my own unique personality with Torah as a guideline.

Yet, sometimes I felt despondent, like everything I hoped for seemed out of reach.

Sometimes I was flying high amid the euphoria of a new awareness or accomplishment that had initially seemed impassable and I was feeling positive and celebratory.

Sometimes I could see the stepping stones ahead to a promising bright future; having my own home and family in Jerusalem didn't seem so far off.

Whatever was going on, amidst the yo-yo moments, I hoped, prayed, believed G-d was with me, there to comfort or cheer me on. I hoped I could be there for myself.

Becoming an *eved* Hashem — a servant of G-d, a person who honors and abides by G-d's Torah, His *mitzvos* and His *halachos* come rain or shine — was indeed a challenge most of the time, but it was satisfying and rewarding enough of the time to prompt me onwards in my quest for a life with new definition and purpose. I knew and lived the alternative and had no intention of backtracking to my secular life back in London — absolutely not.

# 10

Tapping into the potential of Rosh Chodesh became a favorite new pastime when I lived the Jewish Quarter. I was introduced to the uniqueness of Rosh Chodesh and a lovely way to honor it by a flamboyant and friendly young American woman named Tamar, who inspired me to participate in the preparations for her Rosh Chodesh women's gatherings.

Tamar placed sparkling tea-light candles on the pathway to her front door. One light was placed on each of the narrow winding steps that curved up to her roof-top garden apartment that drew you in by its far-reaching bouquet of scents. Tamar was a master at creating a welcoming and beautiful setting for her guests. She dressed every available table-top with a white lace table cloth and exquisite fresh flowers and large scented candles, which gave off a delightful fragrance. She prepared a variety of home-made salads, cakes and refreshments which she laid out with care on fine bone china plates and cake stands, as if she were setting a party for a queen.

Invariably, I went late in the afternoon to help Tamar prepare. While we cut vegetables, decorated cakes or arranged flowers in her large kitchen, overlooking the maze-like streets leading to the Kotel, she gave over teachings about Rosh Chodesh and the ways in which we can pay tribute to this day, in honor of women.

Usually about twenty-five to thirty women would arrive around 8 p.m. Words of Torah were shared by women speakers from all over Jerusalem. Guests were encouraged to add uplifting personal stories of *hashgachah pratis* and some women shared *Chassidishe* tales from books or their grandparents' lives.

The evening's finale was singing songs and *niggunim* — the highlight for me. I felt so close to G-d when we sang together — I didn't want the evenings to end. I love to sing but singing in the group was so very special, it made me feel so happy inside, so connected to my soul. And I know other women must have felt the same way because sometimes many of us forgot what time it was and what we had to do in the morning; we would sing and tell stories of our lives until the very early hours of the morning. None of us wanted to disturb the charm of the night or the unity that had been created among us.

# 11

I n the Old City there was always a woman for me to talk to as I made my way through the narrow, winding streets going to work, to the Kotel, or doing errands. Community life in the Jewish Quarter was *heimish*; if I felt like a chat, I'd drop in on a friend as I passed her home.

I liked this open-door policy; life seemed rosy. However, my morale was weakening, even though I rented a room in an apartment, had a job, went to *shiurim*, and always had nice Shabbos invitations. But after visiting friends or coming back from my job, I would often find myself wandering around at night with a heavy, lonely heart. Often, I would look up at the warm yellow glow radiating from an apartment and hear beautiful clarinet music from within or people in conversation, and I would feel the tears running down my face.

I would see couples in their Shabbos finery walking back from the Kotel, and I would stare with envy; I, too, wanted to be married. Each time this yearning pulled me in different directions; why did I leave behind a potentially good relationship in London? How long will it be until I am ready to marry? How will I get married?

I started to feel real despair and hopelessness. As the days turned into weeks and my feelings of despondency increased, so did my *tefillah*.

# 12

Living in close proximity to the Kotel was the greatest gift of living in the Old City; it afforded me the opportunity to *daven* at any time. Invariably I chose one *tefillah* each day and if I couldn't manage to get there at the right time, I would go there any time to say Tehillim or just to absorb the energy that permeates the Western Wall plaza.

It says in the holy books of Torah that the prayer of every Jew in the world goes through the Kotel before it ascends to the throne of G-d in the Heavens. I used to sit by the Kotel imagining how many prayers had traveled through this holy passageway over the last 3,000 years. Then I sat quietly visualizing the travel pathways of that day's new incoming *tefillos*. When I was in one of my spiritually-open states of being, I realized what an incredible opportunity I was being given to tap into the powerful spiritual energy source that was all around me.

Other days I sat watching the women pour out their *tefillos* to Hashem before the peachy-cream ascending stones that had absorbed millions of feelings and cries of *tefillah* and holy words.

Every observation I have made of a woman or child praying strengthened my bond to G-d and my ability to pray. Some women stood in silent devotion during their structured *tefillah*, praying from a *siddur*. Others freed their spiritual potential through personal expression, talking in their own language. All types of hand gestures accompanied the praying; lifting hands to the sky, placing hands on the heart, wringing of hands, clapping of hands. Everyone, in their own way, was trying to catch G-d's attention — they wanted their *tefillos* to be heard, to be considered, to be accepted.

The Kotel is an awesome place to be at any time of day or night. It becomes more awe-inspiring during Yamim Tovim, or sadly when thousands of people descend on the Kotel to beseech G-d for salvation in very difficult or dangerous times.

An experience that profoundly affected me at the Kotel happened on a spring morning when I was in a questioning mood. My memories have a habit of fading out of view when I need them most. The one that mattered the most that day was the incident with the little Indian baby under the night sky in Uttar Pradesh, the encounter that had prompted me to make a promise to myself to look into Judaism more seriously when I returned from India, but which had been lost in the depths of my consciousness.

I sat on a chair facing the Kotel exposed to the sheltering Heavens. It became obvious to me that G-d could hear all the doubts talking to each other in my head: had I made the right decisions since my first one to adopt an Orthodox lifestyle? The pressure must have been overpowering my rationale, because that day G-d sent a little Jewish girl to help me straighten out my thoughts and life direction, once again.

The air was warm and motionless. I sat with my right hand on the flat ascending stone wall to right my life imbalance of confusion and concern; I wasn't sure how to cope being single in the Old City and I didn't know what to do next with my life.

I opened my *siddur* and tried to focus on the *tefillah*. Just as I was coming to the end of *Pesukei D'zimrah*, I felt a slight pressure on my arm. Looking to my left, I saw a girl, who looked to be six or seven years old. She had maneuvered her way through the crowd and positioned herself next to me. Her mother was bending down next to her and had her arm around her little waist. The girl was wearing an embroidered pale pink linen dress and the mother was dressed in casual white cotton pants with a peach sleeveless shirt and a wispy floral chiffon scarf thrown over her shoulder. The colors were charming in the early morning sun.

"What shall I say, Mummy?" asked the sweet voice of the little Jewish princess.

"I'm not sure. Whatever you want, honey," said the mother.

"But Mummy, I don't know what to say," she continued.

"Here," said her mother and put an open *siddur* into her little hand.

I watched the little girl randomly open the *siddur*. I could see the larger print letters of the Shema clearly in black and white on the page. I was about to *daven* that myself. The conversation was captivating; I had to see how it ended.

"What's this, Mummy?" she said, pointing to the enlarged words.

"It's the Shema, honey; some people say it before they go to sleep."

"I want to say it now. Help me, Mummy. Please, will you?"

The mother took the little girl's right hand and placed it over her eyes and helped her say each word slowly. The little student mimicked the Hebrew sounds.

By now, tears were falling onto my *siddur*.

The images of my experience in India and the whispered promise I made to look into my own legacy appeared like a film reel on the stones in front of me.

G-d felt so near. He had not abandoned me, I had not abandoned myself; I knew what I had to do. I had to return to the start. I had to go back to Har Nof and reconnect and seek counsel. Whenever I am at a crossroads, G-d steps on the road and sends a *shaliach* with clear instructions or reminders of what He expects from me.

"Shema Yisrael..." the little voice repeated her lesson with sincerity, her eyes closed, and her sweet little hand covering her eyes.

After the blessing the little girl sought her mother's approval. She received a hug and stroke on her hair for her efforts. How different this little Jewish girl looked compared to the Indian baby in Uttar Pradesh; how different this little Jewish girl's future would be. How different my life had become since I returned from India and my meeting with the Indian baby nearly two years ago.

I stepped back into my own world and continued *davening*. When I got to the blessings of the Shema, I took more time than usual to prepare myself to have the right intention. I reviewed the last five minutes and said my most meaningful Shema so far in my life.

The following day I had a long talk with a married friend who lived in Har Nof. She offered me her guest room to rent; I took up her offer straightaway.

# 13

I met a woman, Michal, in my first year in Israel, who seemed very special to me. While I lived in the Old City I kept in contact with Michal. I talked to her on the phone a few times a week; her vivaciousness and open-mindedness drew me to her. She was a well-versed guide to single *baalos teshuvah* girls who were acclimatizing to a religious Jerusalem life.

When I moved back to Har Nof to live with the Greenblatts, I told Michal I wanted to start *shidduchim*.

I continued my public relations job in the Old City, leaving the apartment early every morning to get to work on time. It took me a good few months to feel comfortable in Har Nof again. I had returned feeling pretty low and out of sorts. When I left seminary I lost touch with the married women and rebbetzins I had visited regularly when I lived in Har Nof. It was a forty-five minute bus ride from the Old City to Har Nof, too far to go there and back at the end of my busy work day. Now that I was resettled in Har Nof, I felt embarrassed to call up old friends and acquaintances; nearly a year had passed and I was sure they had forgotten me.

During one of my regular conversations with my mother, she commented about the dejection in my voice and said she wanted to visit. How could I say no? I wanted to because I didn't want her to see me in a down mood and attribute it to my new way of life and pressure me to return to London.

Our first few days together were pleasant. We went to the Kotel, had lunch at a bagel café in the Old City and spent the time catching up on all the events in our lives since I left London. We visited some of my married friends in the Old City and ate dinner with one of the families.

On the third day I arranged to meet my mother at the Israel Museum to see an art exhibit. I was looking forward to seeing her; the previous day had gone quite well. Perhaps, if things continued this way, by the time Mum went home she would have a positive impression of my life in Israel. Planning for her arrival had upped my mood; her visit was turning into a good idea after all.

It was raining the day we intended to visit the museum. I left the Greenblatt's apartment without either a raincoat or an umbrella. The taxi I had ordered was waiting outside. It was a ten-minute ride to the museum.

As I went down the stairs to the street to pick up the taxi, I slipped and flew into the air before landing on a steep flight of concrete steps. I recall fear rising as I rose in the air, I recall the immense sound of my first scream, I recall feeling like my soul had left my body when it made contact with the sharp edge of a step.

When I landed, the skies opened and torrential rain drenched me. I lay on the steps screaming, and after what seemed like forever — but was probably five minutes — a man, who had heard my cries, came up the steps. He knelt down beside me and asked me what I felt. I couldn't talk; a shooting pain in my back made me feel nauseous. I couldn't feel my legs.

A few minutes later Mrs. Greenblatt was holding my hand while we waited for an ambulance. It took an hour for the medics to move me; they had to strap me into a body brace. They were amazed I hadn't smashed my skull; they were amazed I was alive — they speculated I had broken my back. I felt a part of me die when they said this; a part of me swooshed up to Heaven: something left me and shot up into the clouds.

My mother sat at the end of my hospital bed in the emergency ward with a contorted face; after a short while I sent her away because the fear on her face was making me hysterical. I still couldn't feel my legs. I didn't know what was going to happen. I experienced the most frightening fifteen hours until I was finally able to hobble out of the hospital with the voice of the doctor echoing in my head: "You are a walking miracle; I just don't understand it."

Bruised and black-and-blue, I lay in the second bed in my mother's hotel room. I hardly moved, my head pounded, I couldn't talk. I couldn't believe I was alive and walking.

In the mornings, my mother tended to my needs and then spent most of the day with my friend's mother, who I had asked to entertain her.

Three days later, on the day of my mother's departure, I willed myself out of bed and returned to the Greenblatts with a bag of new clothes my parents bought for me as a gift.

The following weeks I was in a very dark place: I felt battered from all sides and couldn't see the good in my life anymore. Everything looked bleak; my mother's visit was a disaster, I was in pain all the time, I could hardly speak from the shock of what had happened, I was lonely and bored from being stuck in the apartment for days and days. All I could do was talk to Hashem and ask for His salvation.

A month later, Michal phoned me with an interesting suggestion.

# 14

"Don't tell anyone I suggested this, but I just met a boy who I think you are going to marry," Michal said.

I couldn't believe what I was hearing. Perhaps my *mazel* was changing. Perhaps Hashem had heard all of my weeping and pleas for help, for a miracle, for something wonderful to happen to me. I felt excited. I took Michal's suggestion as a compliment; I thought the secrecy was part of the privilege of her friendship. I listened to her reasoning and I agreed to the *shidduch* without consulting anyone or doing any research on the boy.

# 15

I stood in the hotel lobby waiting for Naftali. My body was still achy from the fall but Michal was eager for me to meet the boy as soon as possible.

I dressed in a mid-blue silk suit with a white shirt. I looked very good. I felt very hopeful. I was desperate. I wanted to start my own life already; I wanted my own husband, my own home. I wanted this so much because I felt I had so little and my personal situation was so hopeless. I had been in Israel for two years and my life was not moving forward. Perhaps this meeting would change everything for the good.

Naftali didn't walk towards me in the hotel lobby where it was arranged we would meet — like most people would have. He came up behind me and smiled at me with a radiant beautiful beam before saying hello.

"You surprised me," I said, referring to his unconventional salutation and approach.

Little did I know what surprises would be in store for me — much later on — from this person who was not who he appeared to be from the start and didn't do things the conventional way.

In the beginning, things went relatively well; our dates were three to four days apart — which according to most Rabbis in Jerusalem was a healthy spacing to ensure an objective perspective of the relationship.

We met in public places, according to Torah law.

Our time together flowed smoothly and our conversations were pleasant — a sign that our relationship was developing nicely. Still, we had not spoken about any "serious" issues like mutual aspirations and money matters, which didn't bother me for some reason, as I assumed one works these things out when one is married.

At the end of one of our dates Naftali escorted me home. I had recently moved into an apartment with a few other single girls. It was a warm spring evening and the stars were twinkling in the sky.

"Let's sit on this bench and talk a little more," said Naftali.

"I'm a little tired, Naftali. Do you mind if we talk another time?" I said, looking at my watch. It was midnight.

"I want to talk more," said Naftali, his voice a bit strained.

"I see that it's important to you, but I have to be up very early tomorrow to get to the Old City by 8:30; I don't think I will be able do it if I stay up any later."

"I said I want to talk more — now!" Naftali screamed.

I looked at Naftali and saw someone else; a person with a temper and a shiver ran through me.

"I have to go home now, Naftali. I am sorry," I said.

Naftali became annoyed and blocked my path. I become very scared and hurriedly walked around him without saying goodnight.

The next day Michal told me sometimes men feel frustrated when they date and this is what happened with Naftali.

"He wants to marry you," Michal said. "He didn't want you to go home."

I didn't see it that way; I told Michal that I didn't want to see this man anymore and I thanked her for the *shidduch* suggestion, but told her that it was not suitable.

# 16

Over the next few weeks Michal pressed me to go out with Naftali again; her argument was so persuasive, the pressure was so intense, her rationale so convincing, I said yes. Before I saw him again after a three-week interval I forgave him for his temper and imagined it was something else, a quality of enthusiasm that showed he liked me.

During the interim I had battled with my feelings; I had liked Naftali but struggled with whether to judge him favorably; and then I concluded: Why not? Wasn't it a mitzvah to judge another Jew in a good light?

During the interim I discussed Naftali's behavior on the first round of dates with one person aside from Michal. This particular rebbetzin was apprehensive about me starting *shidduchim* with him again, but I had already made up my mind to give it second chance. I didn't think of asking her to research Naftali's history or his family background; I had Michal's information and I had gathered my own facts from our dating beforehand. I was relying on my instincts. Not bearing in mind that a girl's instincts — at any age — go haywire on *shidduchim,* was a mistake. My naiveté was my downfall.

When I met Naftali again his passive sweet personality, captivating soft voice and handsome face dazzled me; I didn't realize that I had been caught in a spider's web of infatuation.

I had done something that one should never do on *shidduchim* — let emotions rule the decision-making process. Abandoning logic, I had "closed" my ears to the one person who was adamant I was making a serious mistake when I had described how Naftali acted on our last date before we had a break in the *shidduch*. All I can put it down to is that memory plays games with a foolhardy person. Naftali and I became engaged and married two months later.

Erev Hoshana Rabbah, around three months later, I had to leave our apartment; a third party negotiated a *get* on my behalf; Naftali agreed, retracted twenty-four hours later, and then consented.

Four days later, on a Thursday morning, the rebbetzin who expressed her concern showed her compassion and solidarity; she accompanied me to the *beis din* in Jerusalem.

# 17

The *beis din* office for divorce is a space that hovers between Heaven and Hell; a place where shards of dreams clutter the rooms and the walls have absorbed the wailing of broken hearts.

While Naftali sat outside a consultation room, I sat with a judge and two representatives — the rebbetzin and his rav — and listened to a conversation that I feel freed me to become the person I am today.

"Well, it's obvious they love each other," said his rav.

"I would be interested to know how you can see that?" said the rebbetzin.

"My client said so and you can see how upset she is; she hasn't stopped crying since she got here half an hour ago."

The rebbetzin raised her eyebrows. She shook her head.

"It's trauma. They need a divorce; the marriage is unstable," she said.

"If one party still feels something, then there is hope," said the judge. "Perhaps they could live with a mentor family who could watch over the relationship for six months until they have some marriage counseling."

"I like the sound of that," said his rav. "Let's present this suggestion to him."

While this dialogue was playing itself out, I was sitting in a chair about two feet away. All of the sudden, I felt a strange sensation. It was as if my soul were floating above the room looking down on the situation.

I saw myself looking at myself and a highly-charged wave electrified me. This was *my* life they were talking about; that was me in the story they were telling and the ending they were trying to fix. *Stop! No! I want to write my own ending!* I wanted to shout.

"Excuse me, please. There is something I need to say," I said. My stilted whisper halted the discussion.

"This is my life you are talking about. At the end of day, it's going to be just me and my husband when all of you go home and carry on with your own lives — while I'm still stuck in a bad marriage. I want a *get* today — please."

For the longest moment there was silence.

Within an hour a small white paper fluttered like a pure white butterfly from Naftali's hand into my palm. Naftali had given me a legal document that released me and transformed me into a divorcee — a woman free to begin again.

# 18

Why does a person ask for a divorce in a situation like mine? Wouldn't it have been smarter to keep quiet rather than endure social humiliation and risk never marrying again?

Divorce is an announcement; I failed, I quit, I couldn't make it. But does anyone ever hear the whole story to understand the accounting?

Divorce means both partners become misunderstood people, are going to come out of the situation feeling initially — or in the long term — awful about themselves, perhaps socially rejected, abandoned, and misjudged.

Divorcees don't go around wearing a T-shirt that reads: Treat me nicely; I didn't do anything wrong. Let me be so I can heal myself after this story of shattered dreams ends and I am ready to start over.

A divorcee becomes public property immediately after a *get*, whether she is fortunate to get one straightaway, or in time. Social reorientation for a divorcee is a challenging process, and unsolicited advice adds to the exhaustion. While close friends may know some of the story and be supportive, acquaintances and strangers may not know how to deal with the situation and inadvertently say the wrong thing. Outsiders often take the stance of advice-givers because they feel sorry for you; if you didn't get it right the first time they feel it's their job to help you get it right for the next time.

Keeping Torah Law in the picture can be a comfort; because G-d made a provision for divorce, there must have been a good reason for it. Otherwise, why does divorce exist? Before the world was created G-d knew married men and women would have their challenges and perhaps have to divorce for reasons unique to their individual *tikkun* — rectification for their souls — or their joint *tikkun*.

The question I asked myself in the seconds it took Naftali to walk across the room, where the judges stood watching us, and before he dropped the piece of liberating white paper into the palm of my hands was: how am I going to find out what my *tikkun* is?

# 19

The day I walked out of my former husband's apartment, I knew I would never return. All I wanted that day was to live a normal life.

After I received the official paperwork of my *get* I left the *beis din* in Jerusalem with the rebbetzin. As we walked along the sidewalk in the sunshine she talked about how fortunate I was to have just witnessed an open miracle; "You're free," she said, stopping to look at me. When I turned to look at her, I saw my former husband walking parallel to us on the other side of the road.

*Who is that man*? I said to myself. He was once my husband and now he is a stranger. I don't know him — I don't think I ever really knew him. If I had, I would not have married him.

We walked on and while I listened to the rebbetzin talk about her plans for the day I felt myself going numb.

*Oh my gosh*, I said to myself. *I am back at square one; I am single again.* The reality hit me so strongly I stood still and shook myself to make sure that this wasn't a bad dream.

*Who am I?* I said to myself. *I am not the same person I was early this morning, last week or last year. I am now a divorcee.*

Tears streamed down my face as the rebbetzin led the way forward.

# 20

I felt like I was a damaged person and I needed to heal myself. How would I do it and how long would it take?

A few hours after my *get* I sat with a dear rebbetzin friend of mine in a restaurant; she insisted on taking me out for a fruit shake — she didn't want me to be alone at home. She also felt we had something to celebrate; I was free, and what a gift that would be — when I woke up from my traumatized state.

"Here, take this," she said, passing me an envelope.

I opened it and shook my head.

"I can't take this," I said, feeling a flush of embarrassment rising.

"You left with nothing — just the clothes on your back. Now you have something. My husband and I want you to have this until you get back on your feet."

There was a considerable amount of money in the envelope.

"I will pay you back when I have saved money from a job," I said.

"You don't need to," she said.

I looked into her face and saw genuine friendship and I cried.

I had gotten myself into the marriage — G-d pulled me out — my friends were there to pick up the pieces with me; maybe I would make it, maybe I would get over this, maybe I would get married again and have a normal life, like my friends — maybe I wouldn't.

There are no guarantees after a divorce.

Sunday morning, three days after I was granted a *get*, I was up at 5:30 A.M. After *davening* I paced my room in the home of the Bostoner Rebbe *shlit"a*'s son and daughter-in-law, the Horowitz family, who had sheltered me before my *get* and offered me a place to live afterwards. As I walked up and down, upsetting, fragmented thoughts turned over and over in my mind until the clock showed 6:30 A.M. and I took an hour's bus ride.

I walked along the pathway wheeling two large suitcases. I saw women hanging wet laundry, looking down from their patios, and children passing by, their lunch bags swinging against their knees. These familiar signs came into focus as I entered the home I had shared with my former husband for less than three months.

It had been arranged that my former husband would leave the apartment at 7 A.M. so I could go in and take my belongings. Three friends had agreed to help me pack and would be meeting me in an hour. An hour: all the time in the world to deal with what was in my heart in the aftermath of the storm.

I stood in the living room, in the stillness of a noise that had suddenly silenced inside of me. I looked around carefully looking for any changes but everything was just as it had been seven days ago when I had walked out at 12:40 P.M. on Hoshana Rabbah.

I went into the kitchen; the chicken, potatoes and sweet potatoes that I was cooking for Yom Tov were still in the oven. The knife and the cut up vegetables were still on the cutting board. The sukkah was still standing and the gemara was open on the table.

I walked out into the sukkah, and my heart trembled; the seedlings in the plastic trough had been green plants when we put up the sukkah. I had planted them the morning after our wedding, and now they were in full bloom — orange, red, and pink flowers bursting with vitality. I stood rooted to the spot and sobbed.

What a shame, what a waste, what a mess my life is now.

I continued walking around the apartment. I stood before my former husband's long black silk coat, the *bekeshe* hanging in the guest room. I looked at the fur-trimmed hat, the *shtreimel*, he had donned before the *chuppah*, now on the bed, still elegant and new. I ran the tips of my fingers down the silk and then across the fur and cried.

Death — that is what divorce feels like — death of something once so precious; a loss of something once so dear. That is what our marriage had felt like for a fleeting moment until darkness descended and it was difficult to see the light of anything good and right.

On the mantelpiece in the living room was an envelope: "Dear Leah..."

I read the words and my eyes started raining tears of salt water — I was mourning something that had held so much promise but was rotten to the core.

Divorce rips your heart and soul out — washes them clean and replaces them with a tag attached; fragile, handle with care until the due date — the date you are ready for reclaiming — reclaiming by their true owner — the true intended of this precious person.

Divorce is G-d's way of saying — your mold is too small, I am going to smash it, break it, destroy what I gave you, and then you will have to rebuild it stronger and better and why not a bit bigger, and when you have done your job, I will do mine — I will fill your new vessel with so much *brachah* it will overflow into all areas of your life.

But first you have to take your heart and soul out. Cleanse them — do *teshuvah*; make changes in yourself and your life and promise not to repeat mistakes. Then you have to get your resources together and rebuild a vessel befitting the clean heart and soul. And then you will be ready to reassemble yourself, and when you have done the work that I want you to do, then you will be ready to stand before your other half from Heaven — your true *zivug* — and he will recognize you, and you will go the *chuppah* again and become one again — just as I wanted it to be in the first place.

One hopes this will happen to you but it is not always the case. Many people don't get re-married after a divorce. Many people don't want to do the work they have to do to merit marrying their true *zivug*. Many people re-marry only to divorce again — the cycle of error, disillusionment, destruction and pain repeats itself and leaves its mark on the mind, heart and soul of a person.

When I was divorced, I vowed to be obedient to the words of my spiritual advisors, two of whom had offered me private counseling to work through the trauma, help me work on weaknesses in my character and to learn better positive thinking skills.

I also forgave G-d; initially I was angry with G-d when I woke up from the stupor of my situation. How could G-d have let this happen? It took me a while to come to terms with the fact that G-d didn't let it happen — I did. G-d didn't make the choice for me to marry my former husband regardless of the warnings I had noticed early in the *shidduch* — which I felt, afterward, was G-d talking to me; it was me. I had been a bad listener.

Now I was trying to be a good listener; it wasn't too late. Perhaps the fact that I was free once again meant G-d was going to give me a second chance. If this was the case, I was ready to do the work I had to do and research and consider my options more carefully before I made the next move. Hoping to merit blessing, I also took a vow not to talk *lashon hara* about my former husband.

# 21

After I received my *get* I lived at the home of Rav Mayer and Sima Horowitz. I was so grateful to have somewhere to live — I didn't have a job and I had no savings. I had lived in a different community with my former husband; it took time to feel comfortable again in Har Nof. The Horowitzes eased my transition by treating me like a member of their family, and welcoming me warmly into their day-to-day lives.

It was a wonderful experience to live in a *Chassidishe* home; my soul felt comfortable with this *derech*, way of life. My former husband was *Chassidishe*, and even though some people were a little too quick to comment negatively about my choice, I reminded them — as gently and kindly as I could — that there are good and bad Jews in the world, just like there are good and bad gentiles in the world; being *shomer* Torah and *mitzvos* doesn't "guarantee" one will be a perfectly good person. Following an observant way of life gives a person a framework and a head-start; a person still has to do the work to be good and kindly.

All was quiet in my new status. I kept a low profile in my community; I didn't feel ready to socialize or explain myself. I also stayed close to home, mostly to replenish my emotional reserves; they were below zero after the *get*.

One Thursday, a month later, I popped into Geulah to buy a new Shabbos outfit. I thought this would cheer me up, and seeing as winter had settled in Jerusalem, I was in need of something warmer.

After I had made a purchase of a forest green velvet two-piece —

a new color that I had never worn before — I decided to browse for a matching headscarf. As I walked along the street, a sudden wave of anxiety overtook me. I had this awful feeling that the whole world was looking at me, that they knew my situation, and I felt embarrassed. I hailed a taxi in order to go home, which took me about forty minutes.

When I entered the Horowitzes' kitchen, Rebbetzin Sima leapt up and came over and touched my forehead; I hadn't realized I was scorching red and burning up with a high fever. I collapsed in bed and lay there for four days in a trance-like state; the trauma of my situation had finally hit me. I couldn't talk, I couldn't move — I couldn't believe what had happened to me.

"Come to New York with us," said Rebbetzin Sima the following week.

She was traveling with her daughter to America in a month.

"We'll stay at my brother's in Boro Park. You'll come to my niece's wedding and take me shopping. I need some help with that and you have such a good sense of style. What do you say?"

My eyes brightened as the idea quickly percolated in my mind. Perhaps this was an opportunity to unclip my wings and fly again; this time not to explore the world for travel's sake, but to free myself from a terrible mistake I had just made. Perhaps a friend would lend me the flight money; in the short time I had been living in the house I had earned a little that could cover expenses.

"What a good idea. A vacation will do me a world of good," I said.

Actually, my first thought was: what a great opportunity to run away from my situation.

Later that night I decided a fresh start was the best thing. Within a week I had put all my possessions in a close friend's storage room and was making plans to settle in New York.

# 22

I had forgotten what real winter felt like — winter in Jerusalem was so mild. As I walked out of the airport terminal to find a taxi to take us to Boro Park, I was enveloped by freezing air, which was shockingly exciting.

New York had always held a charm for me; my first trip had been with a friend and her family when I was sixteen. Since then I had been there five more times. Now I hoped that this time would be permanent; perhaps I would stay in New York and make it my home, so I could be far away from my mistake in Israel.

The first few days with the Horowitzes was an adventure; they introduced me to the *heimishe* world of New York shopping as we taxied here and there viewing clothing collections and making purchases for the winter season and in preparation for the big day of the *Chassidishe* wedding of the Grand Rabbi, Levi Yitzchak Horowitz, the Bostoner Rebbe *shlit"a*'s granddaughter.

The evening of the wedding arrived. As we entered the hall in Boro Park I was stunned by the scene; I had never seen so many Orthodox Jewish women in one place looking so elegant and stylish. I felt like I had stepped into a fairy tale; each woman was dressed more beautifully than the next; each woman wore a piece of jewelry more eye-catching than the next.

Black was the dress code, but my eyes beheld black presented in every which way that was exquisite, refined and feminine. Diamonds were the chosen jewel, but diamonds in every shape — with brooches being a popular accessory — and of the finest design and sparkling as brightly as the eyes of the women and the glimmering chandeliers and lights of the *licht* on each table.

The Boro Park *Chassidishe* dress code was worlds apart from the unassuming, feminine clothing and head-covering favored by Orthodox Jewish women in Israel. For weddings, suits, dresses, and separates in all colors were worn with *sheitels*, scarves and hats.

But I never noticed the details of what people wore at *simchos* in Jerusalem; all I cared about was a woman's soul, her substance. And all I wanted to hear were her stories. This is all that mattered to me.

New York was something quite different. It was dazzling and dark and designer label. New York possessed a hint of something reminiscent from my London business life. When I worked in international fashion publicity I flew frequently to Milan, Italy to view the designer and haute couture fashion shows.

Buyers and the press, dressed in exquisite black clothing, sat around the runways watching the runway shows; they were absorbed in the moment; they looked content and beautiful, the scene privileged, glamorous.

Now I was back in a high profile city and I was excited. *If this is the New York Jewish scene, I'm staying.* Part of the "old me" missed the glamour and style of my secular life and after living frugally with my former husband, I was suddenly caught up in a dreamy state of imagination and ambition and a possible change of my prospects, fortune and status if I stayed in America. While admiring this new social set I didn't consider that each woman in the room had a life in New York with its own set of Torah values. I got lost in fantastical aspirations for myself based on first impressions.

Just when I thought my superficial fancy ideas could fly no higher a young girl tapped me on the shoulder: "The Bostoner

Rebbetzin, Raichel Horowitz, would like to talk to you," she said.

I followed the angelic-looking messenger with her taffeta party dress and shiny shoes. As I meandered through the crowded room of women clustered in cliques and chatting among themselves, the Bostoner Rebbetzin, sitting in the corner of the ballroom, came into view. She wore a neat two-piece suit with her *chasunah* trademark accessories — a long row of pearls and an evening hat atop her *sheitel*. I saw her watching me. As I came closer, her smile became wider and brighter.

As I took each step, my new observations and fanciful ideas faded from view, and a simple runway appeared that was fenced on either side with Torah, true simple values reminiscent of the Old Country that I had first heard about from the rebbetzin two years ago when we cooked for Pesach. These had made an indelible impression on me, inspiring me to embrace this way of living.

I could feel myself blushing and becoming upset with myself. In an instant I remembered why I had become an Orthodox woman and what values I was upholding in Jerusalem before I stepped into this wonderful dreamland.

When I was finally standing before the rebbetzin — with the feeling that I just re-lived all the years of my life and all the decision-making processes of the last three years in London and Jerusalem — everything that my mind had been occupied with for the past half hour had been wiped away, and I was once again me, a simple, Torah-true Jewish woman in search of a *pashut*, Torah-true way to live with the partner G-d had designated especially for me.

The rebbetzin enveloped me in a loving embrace and gave me a kiss. She patted the chair and I sat next to her while she asked me to tell her about my visit so far. After our little chat, she said, "I am having surgery in a week. Please come to Boston to look after me for two weeks."

"It would be my greatest joy," I said, as I looked into the Old Country world that seemed to dance in the rebbetzin's eyes, that was the signature of her being.

# 23

I had something important to do before I went to Boston. When I arrived in New York I had phoned Susie, the girl who three years ago had taken me to a *shiur* at Rabbi Simon's home. We had lost touch; I hadn't spoken to her for two years. I still had her number. I decided to surprise her with a phone call.

"Wow! It's great to hear from you, Leah," said Susie. "I can't believe you're calling me today." Her chipper tone bridged the years that had separated us until there was no space at all.

"I'm getting married in two days. I must talk to you; can you come over tomorrow morning? You'll come to the wedding, won't you?"

I whooped with joy.

"Of course I'll come. G-d certainly works in mysterious ways. I wouldn't miss your wedding for the world," I said.

I didn't think for one moment that I wouldn't go to Susie's wedding; I owed her my new life. If she hadn't taken me to the Jewish Learning Center, I wouldn't be an Orthodox woman.

Briefly, I filled Susie in on my personal situation. Then we made plans to meet in Teaneck, New Jersey.

The morning after the *Chassidishe* wedding, a carpet of snow had been fitted on the world. I left New York in a great mood — I love snow.

Susie was waiting in her car at a cross-road by a shopping center in Teaneck.

"I have a million questions to ask you before the wedding," she said. "I can't believe you're here. It's just perfect." She hugged me until I felt like crying. It was indeed a special moment — an amazing coincidence like one reads about in novels.

The rest of the day we talked and talked until we could talk no more. Susie was marrying an Israeli man who had once been Ultra Orthodox and was now more modern — what you might call Modern Orthodox.

The imminence of the wedding had inspired spiritual thoughts in her groom; together, he and Susie had discussed keeping a kosher home. Susie was keen on preparing their new home before the wedding in twenty-four hours. A local rabbi and his wife were on the team, as well as yours truly. It was no easy feat to meet the task within the deadline, but we persevered.

Susie was a good student, even if she looked half-frazzled by the morning of the wedding. By noon, our work was done and she relaxed with the make-up artist. Her family filled the house with piano music to calm her nerves.

When I entered the wedding hall — a banquet suite in a hotel a thirty-minute drive from Susie's family home — I was taken aback. I hadn't thought about anything when Susie invited me to the wedding, the time of year being end of December, or how her modern Jewish wedding would affect me — and here I was standing in a ballroom dressed for the festive season with green fir trees and flashing lights and red velvet ribbons at intervals around the room. A giant shiny silver-colored electric menorah sat on the mantelpiece like a tiara.

Suddenly, I woke up: what sort of wedding was this going to be?

The reception before the *chuppah* was a mixed affair; taking a glass of water, I sat quietly in the corner, drinking in the ambiance.

Susie's parents were famous musicians; the scene was opulent and the height of culture.

While the couple stood under the *chuppah*, her parents played the violin. The dinner and dance was also a mixed affair. Fortunately, there was a table of young cousins, all girls; I sat with them. Susie had kindly ordered me a glatt kosher meal. I ate it with pride; I was determined to make a *kiddush* Hashem — be an ambassador for G-d — at this Jewish, American, Israeli wedding.

My mind flitted between wedding experiences in London and then Jerusalem while I ate my meal. I felt confused and compromised while I saw my friend cutting her layered wedding cake with her new husband before their first dance and everyone else joined in. I was so happy for Susie and I wanted to join in the celebrations because it is a mitzvah to be *mesame'ach* the *kallah*, but Torah Law forbade me from joining the mixed dancing. So, I sat at my table with a pleasant mask on my face, watching all the couples waltzing around the ballroom like a scene from a novel I picked up by mistake.

After about a half an hour, all the guests formed a human caterpillar and danced around the room. As they passed the table where I was sitting, a sprightly man, who looked like he was in his mid-eighties, wearing a rainbow-colored striped shirt and beige pants, kicked his leg in the air and laughed and then cocked his head my way and screeched, "You're missing the time of your life," before bursting into another round of laughter.

"No. I'm not," I wanted to say to him. "This is your life, not my life; mine is back in Jerusalem where I belong." But of course I didn't say this; it wouldn't have been kind or appropriate. Still, somehow these unsaid words made me see who I really was and where I really should be, and I was again grateful to Susie; she had inadvertently helped me see which road to take once more.

Shortly after, I graciously bid farewell to my hosts; I could no longer remain in an environment that was the antithesis of my beliefs.

On my way back into New York I realized that while some Orthodox Jewish women can have a foot in both worlds — the secular and the religious — I didn't have the ability or desire for that dual existence.

I was happy Susie was marrying a Jewish man, but now that I had experienced Jerusalem and I had lived as a religious married woman, I had no inclination to forego my Torah-true commitment in the face of my adversity.

I couldn't backtrack now; it was too late. I was too committed and too sure the way of life I had chosen was right for me.

As the car entered the home stretch into Flatbush, where I was staying with a seminary friend, I imagined myself already in the Bostoner Rebbe *shlit"a*'s home in Boston and I felt agitated; I wanted to be there already, but I still had a few days before I left New York.

# 24

The morning after the wedding in Teaneck, I took a car service to Queens to visit a friend from seminary.

"Where're you visiting from? South Africa?" asked the driver.

"No," I said with a grin. Most people confuse the accents. "I'm an English girl who was living in Jerusalem, now visiting New York."

The driver let out a hearty laugh, obviously amused.

"Aren't you petrified of the Arabs?" His question now revealed his Israeli accent.

"And where are you from?" I inquired knowingly.

"Tel Aviv, but I'm pleased I moved here."

"It's oil and water in Eretz Yisrael," I said. "Arabs and Jews don't mix where I live."

He nodded. He understood.

"Yes, but it's not like that here. There's nothing to worry about, though — I feel safer in New York."

I raised an eyebrow. Now I was amused at his perception. I had never viewed New York as a particularly safe city.

The following day I visited Manhattan's Guggenheim Museum to see an art exhibit and have lunch in an Italian restaurant with another friend from seminary who worked on the Upper West Side.

On my way back to Flatbush, I was the only white woman on the train. I tried to look inconspicuous — impossible, I know — but ensconced in prayer, I *davened* for protection.

A drunkard gets on the train his mouth spewing obscenities. I say *"ein od milvado,"* asking G-d to protect me in the merit of the *segulah* of Rabbi Chaim Vital *z"l*.

The swaying man stands before me but seems to look through me — I feel a streak of fear run through my body and enter my soul — the man stumbles on — I don't start breathing for another few seconds.

G-d is with me — everywhere.

I just realize this for the first time in my life — the awareness reduces me to tears.

# 25

Boston was a train ride from New York and an elegant place where influences of foreign lands flickered before my eyes; the architecture almost English, the design of the streets and the beautifully groomed street foliage and trees reminiscent of elegant Paris avenues, and the onset of real winter carrying the scent and freshness of Swiss mountain air.

I hurry down the street of the Bostoner Rebbe *shlit"a*. I couldn't wait to shelter in the shadow of their wings; my trip so far had been emotionally draining. I wanted to see the rebbetzin, be pampered by her love and get some good sleep.

The inside of the Bostoner Rebbe's Brookline home was old-world grandeur — a sweeping circular central staircase and overhanging square balcony on the first floor were upstaged by a delicate, impressive chandelier that, perhaps, had sparkled in the eyes of the ladies of a bygone era, who had swept down the stairs dressed in beautiful taffeta gowns on their way to a society ball.

I was welcomed with warmth and friendship in the rebbetzin's simple, cozy kitchen, where we talked while we cooked the daily meals and drank cups of tea, discussing life and everything in our hearts.

Over the next two weeks, I shadowed the rebbetzin — helping her with her every deed and every need including pre- and post-surgery — and I believe in the merit of the *chessed* she gave me, I was given as a gift one life lesson after another. Each day was an opportunity to gather and take possession of the rebbetzin's practical, down-to-earth wisdom to strengthen me, guide me, inspire me.

One day, after I delivered a package to the rebbe's study in his shul across the street, I stood for a moment in the main office watching two men, shul congregants, cleaning the rebbe's Chanukah *licht*. It was an antique creation, tall — the height of a four- or five-year-old child — majestic in design, handsome to the eye.

I sighed. Chanukah. Time is passing in America, while life stands still for me in Israel. The afternoon of Chanukah I walked to the grocery store in Brookline. The air smelled clean. I stopped, inhaled deep breaths, and filled my lungs with the pure goodness.

In the gardens, snow was knee-deep. I looked around. I laughed. I counted to three, raised my hands above my head and fell back in the snow; a Jewish star making its mark in Boston. I lay there looking at the grey-white sky. I felt good; new snow makes me feel like anything is possible; the freshness of it energizes me.

I collected what we needed from the grocery store and made my way home past windows where menorahs waited patiently. Chanukah was coming. As I did my own work that afternoon for the rebbetzin I thought about Chanukah and my own memories.

When I was a child I enjoyed staring at our family's small brass menorah, designed in the shape of little dancing men no bigger than the size of my fingers. They seemed to come alive and match the motion of the flickering glow of the brightly twisted tall colored candles.

As my brother and I took turns lighting the menorah on the kitchen counter, my mother and father watched over us. Afterward, it was goodnight and bed.

Over the last few years my relationship with Chaunkah had changed; I now saw it as a meaningful time in the Jewish calendar as well as a happy one. For everyone in Klal Yisrael it provides a unique time, in the spiral of recurring historical events, to express gratitude to Hashem.

The potential of Chanukah was revealed to me for the first time in the preparation classes at Neve Yerushalayim seminary; there we were introduced to the holiday's historical and spiritual essence.

As we learned the *halachos, tefillos, brachos* and songs, I became more intrigued. Past, present and future merged as we were shown how to utilize this time of light and salvation, to brighten the way forward, giving us the courage to overcome all types of challenges and obstacles in life both personally and nationally.

I have fond memories of the first night of Chanukah in Israel. The ten girls in my dorm apartment decided to light our menorahs together. At candle lighting time we gathered in the Neve dining room, along with the whole student body. We placed our menorahs side-by-side. After lighting, we sang together and shared *divrei* Torah and stories over a specially prepared dinner. It was a touching evening; some of us were experiencing our first conscious Chanukah, the rest of the group, religious-from-birth, were away from their families for the first time.

Looking around the dining hall, I marveled at over a hundred menorahs, positioned by the windows, shining out on the world, like beacons in the darkness of the *galus* of our generation.

It was during my first Chanukah in Israel that I first met Harav Chaim Pinchas Scheinberg, Rebbetzin Bessie Scheinberg, Rebbetzin Frume Altusky and Rebbetzin Ruchoma Shain when I had gone to the rav to ask for a *brachah* and advice at this auspicious time.

My second Chanukah in Jerusalem I was living in the Jewish Quarter of the Old City. On the first night of Chanukah, after lighting menorahs with the students on the study program where I now worked, I went for walk into town to Meah Shearim.

Simple homes, reminiscent of Eastern European *shtetls*, lined the narrow winding streets in this part of Jerusalem which appeared untouched by secularization. Sweet sounds of the evening *tefillah* floated out from the *shtiebels*; stepping into Meah Shearim was like stepping in the atmosphere of the Torah world of past generations.

Every so often a front door would open and I would inhale a waft of the pure *kedushah* that permeated from the homes of the *Chassidishe* or Yerushalmi community. The aromas of Yom Tov cooking and happy children's voices floated into the narrow street and left me with a yearning in my heart for a family and home of my own.

Each family expressed Chanukah in its own way. Outside most homes, sitting on a stool or attached to the wall, there would be a glass, brass-rimmed box displaying a menorah for each male member of the family. Some menorahs were gold in color and had a horizontal design with the glass-holders for the oil positioned side-by-side; others were real silver, in the shape of the menorah from the *Beis Hamikdash*, with half-moon curves that connected on a central vertical pillar, reaching up to give their majestic offering to the starry heavens.

My favorite menorah was sitting in a rectangular window of a regular window frame facing the busy fruit and vegetable market. Positioned a safe distance in front of a raised, plain, white lace curtain was a homemade modest menorah; silver foil tea-light containers containing water and golden colored oil had been placed on top of a narrow plank of natural-colored wood. I stood looking at it for a very long time; this sweet menorah shone brighter than all the elaborate and expensive ones. Its message: this was all they had to give, and I felt moved to tears by their contribution. That night I realized that each Jew has something to give G-d regardless of his means and that every effort is cherished by Him.

Chanukah was here again and I was in Boston, and I was hoping for clarity at this favorable time.

# 26

On Erev Chanukah I went with the Bostoner Rebbetzin to the rebbe's study, in the rebbe's shul across the road from their house. The antique shiny menorah had been placed in the doorway, as was the rebbe's custom.

When we arrived, the rebbe, dressed in his silk, black and gold damask Shabbos *bekeshe* and fur *shtreimel*, was sitting beside the menorah, preparing his thoughts; he read from a *sefer*. When the appropriate time arrived, the rebbe lit the candles. I looked into the flames of holy fire. I began to cry a little. The moment was beautiful.

"It is a time to *daven*; this is an auspicious time for you to ask the *Ribbono Shel Olam* for all your needs. The gates of *Shamayim* are open now," the rebbetzin whispered, touching my hand, smiling at me with so much love in her eyes that I wanted to cry some more.

How wonderful to feel the love of another Jew, to feel close to special people who are the epitome of truth, to feel part of a family and a community where I can belong and feel nurtured.

I watch the rebbe *davening*—mesmerized by what I see; I can't believe I am witnessing this moment. I glance at the face of the rebbetzin, who holds a *sefer* in her hands. Her eyes are cast down, her concentration sincere, her heart open wide.

I look into my *sefer* Tehillim — images dance across the page — the wedding in Boro Park, the wedding in Teaneck, the snow-flakes in Boston, me sitting in conversation with the rebbe about my future in his study where paintings and photographs of Jerusalem adorn the walls.

I see myself at the Kotel and the little Jewish princess saying Shema and I forget where I am until I look up at the rebbe *davening* by the Chanukah *licht* and I, too, pray.

My *tefillos* are for peace in the world, for peace in Eretz Yisrael, for peace in Yerushalayim, to be *zocheh* to see the *Beis Hamikdash*, for every girl who wants to become a *kallah*, for every woman who wants to become a mother. I see my dreams on the pages of my *sefer* Tehillim that I hold in my hands; I see my hopes for myself.

Tears wet the pages — each drop like a snowflake — pure and from the source of my being. I yearn to return to Jerusalem, to become a wife, a mother, to live as a Jew in the land of my people.

The plane touches down — the air on my face is warm, the sky a brilliant blue. My heart is racing. I am home; back home in the land of my dreams.

# 27

I went from Ben Gurion Airport straight to the Horowitz home where I was invited to stay as long as I liked. The week of my return from America I was fortunate to get a job teaching *aleph-beis* and *parshah* to children through art and creativity.

It had been the Bostoner Rebbe *shlit"a*'s idea to work with children. While discussing my options in the rebbe's study in Boston a few days before I left for New York, the rebbe had suggested I use my creative skills to earn a livelihood when I return to Israel. The rebbe blessed me that I should find a good job and hoped I would work with children because he felt that would be fun and rewarding and would prevent me from getting too serious about life.

My new boss operated a private kindergarten; she was looking for a creative teacher to do one-on-one work with children between the ages of three and five.

I loved my new work; it was like a breath of fresh air in my life. Until this time I had never worked with children and I missed my creative pursuits from my childhood years when I had a natural flair and a great passion for photography, water-color painting and drawing. Now I was doing something I enjoyed in a country I was happy to call home.

A year later, one of my student's parents suggested I rent my own apartment and loaned me the deposit. I moved into a freshly painted home with a mattress a friend had given me as a gift. For a week that was all I had and it felt lovely to finally have a place of my own.

I established the Art Club, an afternoon art school for children, a month after I moved to Brand Street, an eight-minute walk from the Horowitzes. From these simple earnings I was able to pay rent and buy groceries.

It was wonderfully cathartic to have the apartment "come alive" with creativity and the happy sound of young children; for two years I dedicated myself to their growth and development.

Under the Bostoner Rebbe's advice I attached myself to an art therapist with a PhD who mentored me in the principles of a remarkable therapy, which I was able to weave into private art classes.

In this way, I was able to help many children overcome significant traumas and challenges where other professionals had been unable to meet with progress or success.

*Teaching the children of Har Nof, under the auspices of the Art Club, allowed me to give something of worth to my community; the children's presence in my home also brought me much happiness and helped me reclaim a sense of purpose and self-worth.*

Moreover, I was able to also heal myself and start to feel good about the future. Giving to others helped me overcome past disappointments; giving filled my life with purpose and satisfaction and joy.

Shabbosos I spent with either the Har Nof Bostoner community — the Bostoner Rebbe and Rebbetzin lived in Jerusalem for six months out of the year, when they weren't living in Boston, Massachusetts — or new friends on Brand Street.

I was never alone on Shabbos. I wanted it that way. My feet hardly touched the ground from Sunday morning to Motza'ei Shabbos. I made sure to keep myself busy. I didn't want to think. I didn't want to be pulled back into the past. I didn't want the possibility of a bright future to be hindered by anything negative that might appear if I spent too much time thinking and worrying about my mistake, my error of judgment, my former marriage.

# 28

My greatest source of strength after the divorce was my relationships with my beloved rebbetzins. Almost all of them were women decades older than me who I had met in my first year in Israel. Rebbetzin Bessie Scheinberg, Rebbetzin Ruchoma Shain, Rebbetzin Raichel Horowitz and a new "guiding light" Rebbetzin Yehudit Soloveitchik, the wife of Rav Dovid of Brisk Yeshivah were all my teachers, mentors and role models, whom I tried to visit weekly.

Rebbetzin Soloveitchik learned with me once a week in her "Old Country" home that reflected her values, all of which appealed to me in every way for their honesty, grace and truth without fanfare or wasted finance. She gave me good advice on re-entering the *shidduch* world.

In spite of her tutelage, the first year after the *get* I took one day at a time and each day was productive, satisfying but also extremely painful.

I hated being divorced; it wasn't the embarrassment that pained me so much — the shame of being single again and what people might be thinking about me — it was the loneliness and the loss of an expectation that caused me the most anguish.

Even though I conducted myself with confidence — I kept a nice home, I was doing well with my work, I dressed neatly and I gave the impression of being content and grateful for my lot in life because I genuinely felt that way deep down — I disliked looking like I was married. I still covered my head with a *sheitel*, as is customary for a religious Jewish woman after marriage. But in my heart, I felt like a fake, like I wasn't being a truthful person. It was my choice and it was the right choice, but it was still hard — to look married and not be married.

The day of my *get*, after I said goodbye to the rebbetzin who had accompanied me, I had gone to see Harav Chaim Pinchas Scheinberg for some words of inspiration and to ask the rav some questions about personal conduct.

When the rav saw me, he raised his hands to the Heavens and cried with me; the rav said there wasn't much to say to console me except he made me a promise — he said if I kept my head covered — with a *sheitel* outside the home and a scarf or snood in the home — I would merit marrying a *ben* Torah.

As always I followed *daas* Torah; I wanted to merit this blessing. I was willing to do whatever it took to gain G-d's favor.

Before I left his home, Rabbi Scheinberg asked me to come and see him every week; he counseled me like a father lovingly guides his child after a fall. His words were helpful, thoughtful, and optimistic: *be patient; your time will come.*

I was patient; there was no choice, but the rav made it easier for me to play the waiting game.

# 29

The days are running into each other; I work night and day to avoid the pain, avoid being conscious of my state, avoid being pulled back into the past.

I rise early, take my time *davening* with as much *kavanah* as I can muster, begging G-d to notice me today, to help me, to carry my burden with me. I dress with care and walk to work, leaving the Horowitz house around 7:30 A.M. to get to the kindergarten where I work half an hour later.

I take a slow walk through the community that is familiar to me. I know people on every street; I have a memory bank of experiences for every day I have been in Har Nof. I am back where I started when I arrived on Sunday 15 August 1993; I am single, searching and praying for a miracle.

The days in the kindergarten on Rechov Agassi are pleasant and rewarding. From the moment I arrive I am occupied, actualizing a creative curriculum I formulated to teach the sixty three-to-five-year-olds *aleph-beis* in small groups and one-on-one. My new boss has given me a corner that I can call my own. Each week I decorate it, making it colorful and intriguing so the little people, my new friends, feel comfortable in my space while we learn together. The Gold Book is the title of the project for the year. Each week each child spends time working with me filling their personalized Gold Book with imaginative work related to the curriculum. I love my work; it is happy and purposeful and fills me with peace.

The day rolls on; all afternoon until early evening I go from house to house up and down the mountain of my community. I visit students for whom I have created a tailored arts and crafts program with a personalized purpose. One child learns patience through their projects; another how to listen, yet another how to be free to be himself. Once again I am stepping into other people's lives and capturing a glimpse of another person's reality. Once again I am a voyeur, a student of life, an anthropologist.

Wet days, sunny days, chilly days, windy days, my schedule is the same as is the tune; keep busy, don't think, earn money to live, smile — no one has to know how hard it is. I know the tape recording in my head by rote; you cannot go back to London, there is nothing and nobody there for you anymore, it is not the place for you, it never was, you have to stay here. Then the second voice: But what will become of you? Will you remarry or will you be doing this forever? There is no choice; without money you can go nowhere. I hate this recording, but there is no other, even after the weekly counseling from Harav Chaim Pinchas Scheinberg *shlit"a* and Rabbi Zelig Pliskin *shlit"a*, whose self-help books had inspired me — even after I don the mask of happiness and loveliness.

I force myself to be happy, to be positive. I work hard at being successful; I have to be victorious. There is only me now and I must make something of myself.

But one day the mask tumbles down. I cancel my afternoon appointments, go back to the Horowitzes because I feel sick with my life; I have a fever; I am slipping into a very bad place. I don't want to be divorced. I don't want this reality. It is 3 P.M. The phone is ringing as I enter the house.

"Grandma died," says my brother.

I cannot speak; I don't believe it.

"She wasn't feeling well three days ago; she was in hospital. She died an hour ago."

"Why didn't you call me? I could have spent some time with her. I could have said goodbye. She was my grandmother; I loved her, too. Why didn't you tell me?"

My brother doesn't answer; he knows the answer he has will be wrong for me to hear. I've known my brother twenty-nine years, and I can read him like a book — it has the similar jacket to my parents' — but I hope that one day I will find a different story inside.

"Don't come for the funeral tomorrow; it's not a good idea," he says, the only time he has alluded to my new status, the first time I am speaking to him since the divorce.

"She was my grandmother. If I want to come to the funeral, I will," I say, wondering why my brother tends to forget I am the oldest and it's not appropriate for him to tell me what to do, unless I ask.

I need to get off the phone; this conversation is getting me nowhere. I need to move into gear. I phone the Rolls in London; their home is open to me.

Within forty minutes I am speeding down the Tel Aviv highway with my boss and her husband; in my hand is the $1000 they handed me when they came to collect me, to pay for the flight and to get me through my days in London. The British Airways stewardesses are so kind and compassionate. I finally cry.

At London Heathrow I phone my mother; it's midnight.

"It's me," I say.

"I knew you'd come," she says. "Be here tomorrow morning at 9 o'clock to go in the car with us," she continues.

I tell her where I'm staying; she says, "Good."

I look around me; if I scream I wonder who will notice.

Rabbi Roll and Julie are waiting up for me. They open their hearts to me as I pour out my story since the *chuppah*. I love them for being my friends, for listening, for being in my life.

The grey stone funeral parlor is freezing, the icy January wind seeps through the old wooden windows. Friends of my parents and a few distant cousins huddle down one end of the room. I stand opposite Dad and my brother. I stand next to my mother. My Dad's sister is next to Mum on the other side. Grandma is between us in a pine coffin, silent, forever gone from my life.

But now my Grandma knows the truth; she was so happy when I got married. I phoned her every week, but in the end decided not to tell her I had to get a divorce. From where she is now she can see the truth. I cover my face in shame. I sob behind my hands. My weeping is unbridled; I am the only person crying out loud. My mother nudges me with her elbow.

"Shush, shush. Don't cry like that," she says, but I cannot stop myself.

I weep so loudly she nudges me again.

*My beloved Grandma, early 1930's.*

*Grandma, I am sorry. I wish I could have said good-bye. Now you know the truth.* I say these words in my head and feel the room filling with all the lovely hours we talked and she listened and I felt enwrapped in her love.

I am looking at my grandfather's headstone for the first time; seeing our family name — Warshawsky — for the first time. A red fox peeps its head out from the behind the head stone. I think of the story in the holy books of Torah that tells of Rabbi Akiva's laughter after witnessing the destruction of the *Beis Hamikdash*. When he arrived at the Temple Mount he noticed a red fox running out of the place where the Holy of Holies had been. His accompanying scholars had begun to tear their clothes and cry, while Rabbi Akiva laughed. The scholars asked why he was laughing to which he replied, "Why are you crying?" He went on to explain that the red fox was a sign that the prophecy of the Jewish redemption would be fulfilled. I gasp. I think of Yerushalayim *Ir Hakodesh*, my new home and realize Hashem is here with me; He is telling me not to worry, that my choice is the right choice, that it is best for me in Eretz Yisrael. I perk up, I stand taller. My father notices the shift and eyes me curiously.

As we walk back to the car, my father walks in pace with me.

"The rabbi who read the eulogy," he says, "Mum dated him before me; he might have been your father. You'll probably marry a rabbi because Mum nearly did," he adds.

I answer, "Amen." It seems appropriate.

Dad walks off. My brother follows. Mum is already in the waiting car. I look out onto the vast, desolate cemetery. An eerie silence unnerves me; death seems so close. Then I saw him again, the red fox looking at me from behind another headstone and I remember, I remember who I am, where I have come from and where I shall return.

My parents' elegant living room in their West End apartment is jam-packed with people; I can hardly move. Encircling me and my brother are all my brother's friends from his English boarding-school days, all the boys who were like brothers to me when I was growing up, about ten of them, chatting to my brother while I look on.

Suddenly, a voice screeches like a wild bird across the room and

the roomful of about a hundred guests goes silent, waiting for a re‑
ply. My grandmother's sister, Lily, has called my English name and
then asked me, "What's it like living in Israel with your husband?
Grandma was so proud."

As I take in her expectant face, my eyes shift instantly to my fa‑
ther sitting next to her. I feel like I am hovering before an iceberg;
a cold chill runs through me. I allow myself to float on; hoping a
nod will suffice and my parents will not be shamed. It is better I
carry the shame for it is, indeed, my responsibility.

Five minutes later, the rabbi of our family shul in Hendon ar‑
rives. My brother and I are called over by my father to pay our re‑
spects; it has been a very long time since my brother's bar mitzvah,
but the rabbi remembers us both and gives us a kindly smile and
a good word.

"You must be so proud to have a daughter married to a nice
*frum* boy living in Yerushalayim, *Ir Hakodesh*," says Rabbi Moshe
to my father.

My father is forced to do the nodding now while I look away
and imagine my grandmother's face and feel my face flush with
shame and the tears emerging.

I travel back to the Rolls' house in a black taxi; it is evening,
and it is raining. In a few hours I will return to the airport. I lay
my head on the window and look out at the cold, dark London
night. I feel utterly alone in the world. The feeling is so awful I
start sobbing, I cannot control myself. I hear a bell tinkle. I look
up. Hanging on the driver's mirror is a hand-embroidered triangle
with three words stitched on it just for me: GOD LOVES YOU.

# 30

For a year I tried to heal my pain, come to terms with my new reality.

I *davened* to G-d.

I cried to G-d.

I wrote to G-d.

I begged G-d for a second chance.

I worked on refining myself, hoping that in the merit of my efforts I would be blessed with a good husband.

I worked on my faith and trust in G-d; I studied the Torah sources about it; I talked to women about it; I tried to get a grasp on the fact that if I had faith and trust in G-d I could let go, and let G-d do His work; let Him run my life according to His plan for me.

It was tiring work — letting go, relinquishing control, pulling up from the root deep strands of belief that I was in control of my life and my destiny, but I wanted a second chance. I needed a miracle.

After a year of serious personal introspection and particular developments in my character and outlook on life, I followed the advice of the Bostoner Rebbe *shlit"a* and *davened* for forty days at the Kotel; the Rebbe said it was a *segulah* for the thing you are *davening* for. I *davened* for a healthy, kind and gentle husband.

When I began going to the Kotel a euphoria overtook me. It is the most auspicious place for a Jew to *daven* and when you are pouring out your heart to G-d each and every day and anticipating it each and every day on the bus journey there, a certain feeling enters your heart when you finally lay your head and hand on the comforting, steadfast wall of the Kotel.

But as each day passes one's *kavanah* transforms from asking G-d to bless you to a heartbreaking plea and the shift makes you tremble to the very core. On the fortieth day at the Kotel I stood begging G-d for my true *zivug* — the day was the anniversary of my first wedding.

That night, I waited up until dawn for a meeting with a certain *Chassidishe* rebbe whom I was told would be able to help me with my *teshuvah* process — with deep rooted spiritual rectification — my personal *tikkun*.

I had decided my divorce was G-d's way of saying I had made a mistake — that I needed to refine myself, fix parts of myself that were in bad shape, that I needed to become a better person before He would bless me properly. I interpreted my divorce as G-d's way of saying, "You've got more serious work to do on yourself, and this is the way you are going to do it; I'm going to break you and you will have to rebuild yourself to my new specifications and then I will grant you what I want to give you."

In the year since the *get*, I felt I had gone as far as I could with the help of my spiritual advisor, but I was worried. Nothing was happening. I felt stuck. I did not have the confidence to start *shidduchim*. I sensed something more had to be done but I didn't know what. A close friend who had a similar feeling about another type of personal challenge suggested I talk to a particular *Chassidishe* rebbe who had a reputation to see beyond the heart of a Jew and into his soul, to see what had to be fixed. I was apprehensive, I was nervous, but I wanted blessing, so I was ready to listen and to do whatever the rebbe told me to do.

It had taken me months to get an appointment with this particular rebbe. I was amazed when I had been given a time to meet him that coincided with my last day at the Kotel. I had much anticipation while I waited in the rebbe's home at 6:30 A.M.

I sat humbly before the rebbe. He asked me what I wanted. I asked, "What should I do to merit finding my true *zivug*?"

The rebbe listened to my short question and gave an answer: a list of eight tasks designed especially for me; a list of *chessed* tasks I couldn't imagine doing.

The rebbe explained each task. I wrote everything down carefully so I would not forget one detail of the instructions. He told me when I complete the list of particular tasks, I will meet my *zivug*, my true life partner. I believed him. He told me G-d had not abandoned me; that G-d loved me; that I should have faith in G-d's plan for me.

That morning, as I walked away from the rebbe's home, I became more of a believer.

I wrote this piece after I completed my first task from the list the rebbe gave me.

## *Chessed* for My Soul

I must have paced up and down the sidewalk about twenty times before I was able to walk in the building. As the buses whizzed by and the humidity threatened to create more droplets of perspiration on my brow, in my mind I replayed the meeting and the list the rebbe had given me, over and over and over again. Do acts of *chessed*. Help an elderly woman. That was the first assignment on an agenda of eight, just for me. The words rang in my ears, droning on, pushing me forward. I was here, wasn't I? But why couldn't I make it across the threshold? Only the Rebbe knew.

Finally, after half an hour of pounding the stones in the wildly hot morning sun, I thrust open the heavy glass and wooden door and entered the reception area. I looked around. The space was sparse. The floor was so shiny and squeaky clean you could almost make out your reflection in it. The worn sofas looked comfortable. The smell of hospitals and aging mingled and lingered in the air.

A small-faced woman greeted me from behind a huge desk.

"I'd like to volunteer."

"Along the corridor to the green door on the right. Ask for Sarah. She's the one to speak to," she said.

I followed her directions and found Sarah. She and her colleagues were sorting pills and chatting about the weather. Drop, drop, drop, the sounds of the pills hitting each other in their plastic containers could have harmonized with an orchestra of dainty raindrops, if it had been raining. The opposite was true. We were experiencing a typical Middle Eastern summer but by now the water beads on my forehead had been washed away by cool waves from the air conditioner.

"We have someone you could help. It's up to you. She happens to be one of our most challenging of residents."

Sarah's honesty didn't frighten me. I took her suggestion as a sign from Hashem, one of opportunity; after all, who said the merit of *chessed* comes from doing easy acts? I nodded my head.

Sarah gave me a quizzical look. "You don't by any chance have time to help now? An hour to help Mrs. Reich today?"

I nodded again and then stepped into her footstep marks on the carpet as she led me down a narrow corridor, which had doors every twenty yards or so.

"Here's Mrs. Reich's apartment. Number 18." Sarah indicated with her outstretched arm. The skin on her hand was pale, the years of her life in the crevices of her wrinkles. A closer inspection might reveal her age to someone who has knowledge of such things. Her face perplexed me. The window to her soul seemed ageless. Wrinkleless. Pleasant and sweet. It shone in the dim hallway like a beacon in the night. The effects of *chessed*, no doubt.

Sarah's hand scrunched to make a fist that tapped lightly on Mrs. Reich's door.

"Come in!" boomed a manly voice.

Sarah and I exchanged glances. *"Hatzlachah rabbah.* Come see me after," she said in a very small voice as she turned the doorknob and gestured me inside.

For a fleeting moment it felt like Sarah was leading me into the lion's den. I felt vulnerable. Could I cope with the encounter? The magnetic voice repeated itself. It drew me in. I entered a little space with just enough room to house a single bed, two moon-shaped fabric chairs, a sideboard cabinet that ran the length of one wall and a centrally positioned hexagonal wooden table that served as an all purpose surface. The cream curtains were swept back and held in place by twisted silky cords. The open windows revealed an uninterrupted view of a lush green valley that dipped deep into a forested ravine. My eyes immediately scanned the breathtaking view before returning to the foreground.

It took me a few moments to absorb the grandeur of the one room apartment. The walls were painted soft peach and were adorned with exquisite art, mostly of landscapes and flowers. Each painting was dressed in a gold ornate frame. Crystal vases filled with fresh roses stood at intervals along the sideboard in between silver-framed photographs and porcelain figurines. Mrs. Reich's external world was picture perfect and the epitome of femininity. Mrs. Reich herself was exactly the opposite. Perched on a haphazard bed, the bedcovers crumpled and stained, with scrunched used tissues covering the top sheet like a light layer of snow on a below zero day, sat a hugely obese woman. Her drab housecoat was as sad as the face that looked at me from behind expressionless inky black eyes.

"*Oy vey*," I said to myself. "What have I gotten myself into?"

I introduced myself and told her why I had come.

"Sit down. I'll tell you what to do when I am ready."

Her reply hung in the air until after about ten minutes she gave me an instruction. More like a command than a gracious request. Mrs. Reich told me to take her off the bed and undress her. She wanted to have a shower. I looked at her and shuddered inside. I was tall but not that strong. Could I do it by myself?

I stood and put one step in front of the other, willing myself to do the job asked of me. It was a struggle. So intimate a task and so far from what I wanted to do. I bent my knees and inhaled a deep breath, taking the weight of the load on my hips; I lifted Mrs. Reich and did her bidding. I held my breath throughout the endurance. My nostrils had flinched closed at the hint of the smells hovering over her skin. Slowly, slowly each layer of soiled clothing was peeled away and dropped on the spotless peach carpet. Mrs. Reich shuffled to the bathroom and I was left alone. Before she entered the bathroom she turned her body toward me and shot me some words.

"Sit there. Don't move. Wait for me."

And I did. My thoughts encircling me like vultures hungry for prey. My deliberations were that desperate, they practically destroyed my desire to honor my Rebbe's words.

After what seemed like hours, Mrs. Reich emerged fresh as daisy but as miserable as a crushed dandelion.

"Put this on me," she told me, pointing to a nightdress that had seen better days.

Soon Mrs. Reich was lying in bed, reading and intermittently checking my presence with weary eyes. Each stare looked like it was exhausting her. *You can trust me*, I wanted to say, but didn't dare. I sat again for the longest minutes until her next instructions, which came like quick punches.

"Do this. Now do that. Do this. Now that and now this."

I was moving quicker with each task. Exhausted and confused, I was dismissed an hour later without a superfluous word.

"I think it was a disaster," I summarized to Sarah.

"We'll see. Could you come back next week if she wants you to?"

"I can't imagine she will, but yes, I could come the same time next week."

My commitment forced open my mouth releasing words that feigned gratitude. I was trying my best. The mask was effective. I could only manage because I envisioned ripping it off when I got home.

"Call me later and I'll tell you what to do," Sarah decided.

After the mask was safely put away in the drawer in the living room of my quiet home, I called Sarah. It was three hours after our conversation.

"She wants you to come back. She even smiled when she told me. I can't believe it," Sarah said, bewildered. "It's the first time she has said that about any volunteer. What did you do?"

"What she asked," I said truthfully. "Nothing more. Nothing less."

"How did you know to do that with her?" Sarah's question was genuine; she was seeking solutions to collect for tomorrow's challenges.

"She gave me the key," I admitted. "After sitting for the first ten minutes in a void of silence, she reached over and grabbed my right hand, practically squishing the life force out it, staring at me with eyes that made me scared to move or think.

"Then Mrs. Reich handed me the key: Give a person what they need, not what you want to give. 'Do what I say when you are here.'" I was so desperate for the mitzvah that I was able to surrender to Mrs. Reich's need — her will — accept my decree, and struggle in silence as my *neshamah* did its *tikkun* in the hope of winning G-d's favor.

# 31

W hat does *chessed* do for me?
It helps me forget about myself and give to others. It trains me to give when I don't want to give. It is making me into a more patient, understanding, compassionate person, and it is making me into a better listener. I always imagined I was this type of person and perhaps I was intrinsically, but to be a person with these character traits *one has to use them*.

I spend the next year doing the eight tasks the rebbe gave to me.

# 32

By the time I had been divorced a year I had sat in many lectures, read many books, and had many conversations — that all pointed to the same fundamental facts — the heart of Torah belief is:

G-d is the Master of the Universe.

A person's success is due to G-d's Divine will.

That G-d comes before me and I exist to serve Him using my free will.

Faith and trust in G-d's ways will help me achieve what I was created to achieve and undergo the challenges I was created to endure.

Where is there room for me to maneuver in this Divine list; to embrace opportunities that could influence a positive change in my destiny?

I was working out this answer by living the answer. In the beginning I was a girl born into a traditional secular Jewish family, then I was a working girl trying to climb the success ladder, then I was a world traveler in search of truth, and then I was a Jewish girl who surrendered herself to the will of G-d and who was restructuring her life so she could live as an Orthodox Jewish woman (albeit divorced at this point in the story).

By making G-d's will "my" will, by putting G-d and His Torah above me — which is what the rebbe's eight tasks helped me do — I felt a shift take place in my life, which I prayed would, in turn, affect my destiny.

There was no secret to what I was doing; it was hard work based on pure faith — a surrender of my will for G-d's will, a surrender of secular values for Torah values, a surrender of what I felt I could do for what the rebbe said I should do to merit my true *zivug*, my life partner. And the hard work was just beginning — the eight tasks were teaching me essential Torah life skills — and I prayed it would be worth it in the end.

And what would have happened to me after my divorce if I hadn't honored my commitment to G-d, have done sincere *teshuvah*, dedicated myself to the spiritual rectification as advised by the rebbe, and have been patient?

I may have given up on G-d.

I may have abandoned my Torah life.

I may have rejected the rectification plan and married the next man who came along without doing the work I had to do.

I may have decided never to get married again because I doubted my ability to make good decisions.

Thank G-d I have a different story to tell.

I didn't give up. I wanted a life of truth and I was prepared to do whatever it took to find the truth. When I found it I didn't regret the past; I embraced the present. I attached myself to G-d and His Torah, trying my best to emulate His ways in my own way and believe what I was doing was right for me. I knew I had taken a wrong turn in life, I had to start over.

It's not a simple thing to make changes in life, to walk a new path after a life-altering test that shows you the way you were doing things was wrong. I found the whole experience humbling and in some ways quite exciting, but only when I came out of the darkness and was able to visualize a brighter future.

A person never needs to walk the path of life alone. A person can ask for guidance and help from an expert, a mentor, a friend or someone who has experienced something similar and is willing to share their story and offer a helping hand.

Writing was among one of the "best friends" that helped me. Each day of the twenty-four months that I was divorced felt like a year; the time went very slowly and I filled it up the best I could, but the nights were the hardest.

Alone in my apartment I cried to G-d begging Him to change my life; I wanted to be a wife; I wanted a partner, a companion; I didn't want to be alone.

Even though I had a personalized to-do list and *brachah* from a *Chassidishe* rebbe I took on extra tasks hoping to speed up my salvation. I *davened* daily specific *tefillos* as a *segulah* — I read *Shir Hashirim*, the Ramban's Letter and particular Tehillim; monthly I *davened* at the graveside of holy *tzaddikim*, beseeching G-d, in the merit of the righteous people who were now dead, to consider my prayers for salvation; I sought out rabbis and rebbetzins for blessings; I gave *tzedakah* generously — twenty percent — during this time; I did as much *chessed* as was humanly possible beyond the rebbe's list; I made an extreme effort to look my best, dress my best, and think, speak and act my best. Maintaining my faith and trust was a twenty-four-hour job.

*Baruch* Hashem, after living with the Horowitzes for a year, I was able to rent an apartment. Having my own space to think and create eased the burden of my life. I stopped going to families in the afternoon to teach. While I honored the rebbe's list, I was building a new life of my own. I even initiated a Summer Art Camp in the summer of 1995 for forty girls between five- and thirteen-years-old; we had a great time learning drawing techniques in the Jewish Quarter of the Old City, water color skills in the Jerusalem Forest, and sculpture clay methods in my apartment. Waking up to a wall gallery of my students' creative work gave me impetus to continue, to stay living in Israel, to manage the waiting game that G-d was asking me to play. Yet, as busy as I made my life, I could never completely forget my reality.

A June afternoon — the day of my second wedding anniversary — I walked into Harav Chaim Pinchas Scheinberg *shlit"a*'s study with tears coursing down my face. Everything that was seemingly going well in my life — with the new home and the Art Club — that day was suddenly relegated as I tried to tell my rav what had happened.

The night before I had been at a splendid *Chassidishe* wedding and had left the wedding hall at the end of the evening feeling like a forlorn waif; I had stumbled home, hysterical. I wanted to be married. I hated being single again. Going to weddings was becoming harder and harder. Living behind a mask of acceptance and capability and upholding an image of grace and self-assurance was draining me to the core.

I said to the rav: "You have to do something. You have to talk to G-d. I can't wait much longer. I don't think G-d can hear my *tefillos*; but yours, He will certainly hear. *Daven* for me, please, I beg you. I feel like an orphan; I don't have parents or a friend looking out for me, who will help me find a husband and get married. At this moment I feel utterly alone; I feel I have nothing and I have nobody."

Rabbi Scheinberg was used to my soliloquies; for the last four years while I had been a *bat bayit* in his home, he had accepted my honest, direct ramblings, which invariably started off our many conversations about faith and trust and my past life and my future prospects.

Yet this time, my rav, my spiritual mentor, my counselor since my divorce, looked at me with an appearance of complete surprise on his face.

"I don't understand you," he said, genuinely shocked. "Hashem is your Tatty and Mommy." He spoke the truth, his truth and also mine; a truth I tend to forget in my most challenged times. The rav calmed my hysterical soul with seven words: "Hashem will provide; a little more patience."

He then told me to go and talk to the rebbetzin.

"It won't be long now; a little more patience. I promise you," the rav said.

I trusted him; I became more patient. I had to for my general health, if not for my spiritual well-being.

It was nearly two years since my *get*. I was beside myself with worry; would I ever marry again? Many people told me worry is a sign I didn't have trust and faith in G-d. I felt I did but I still worried.

I had worked through the list the *Chassidishe* rebbe had given me, yet something was bothering me; emotionally I felt a block of some sort. I worried this was holding back my *brachah*.

# 33

Where were my parents during this time of my life?
This is a complicated question for me to answer but I will answer in the best way I can because if you ask my parents they will, of course, have a different answer to what sometimes happens to children who relinquish a secular life and take on a life of Torah and *mitzvos*. I am writing these words because, perhaps, someone reading this book will be comforted by my tale and gain strength from its ending.

I gave my parents no joy when I married my former husband, an American Orthodox Jewish man who was a *cheder* rebbe. He was not what my parents had in mind for a husband for me; they were deeply disappointed with me after they met him a few days before the wedding.

Very early in the morning, three months later and two days before I was scheduled to receive a *get*, against a stern recommendation from the rabbi advising me at the time, I phoned my parents out of some sort of obligation I felt I owed them. I told them I had something important to say, could they both come on the phone line.

"I am sorry to tell you some sad news," I said.

The silence urged me on; I was shaking while holding the receiver.

"Naftali wasn't so nice to me; I am getting a divorce."

It was eight in the morning English time — a four-and-a-half-hour plane ride away.

"Do you have anything to say to your daughter?" my father asked my mother.

"No," she said.

"You made your bed, young lady; now you have to lie in it," my father said, and the phone line went dead.

I looked out of the window of the room where I had made the call. The view from Rav Mayer Horowitz's study was pleasant; a birch tree stood tall and grand outside on the sidewalk of their driveway, its leaves wearing golden and brown shades of autumn. The house was quiet; Rav Mayer and his wife were out of town.

I stared into space, into a panorama of images that fogged and then became intermittently animated. I saw all the days of my childhood, and all the days since I arrived in Jerusalem, and I cried. I had made a few bad moves. All I wanted was compassion, a good word, a helping hand, and there had been silence.

I saw my parents' faces in my mind's eye and I looked into their hearts and I knew then, like I have always known, that my parents didn't have the capacity to give me what I truly needed, and that is why I have always sought what I needed elsewhere.

I saw myself in my imagination saying to my parents:

"It's okay; I see you can't help me. If you could you would. I know you are doing the best you can with the resources you have, and that you are limited just like I am limited, just like every person is limited. You are still my parents and I accept you for who you are."

And then I let go of every expectation I have had of my parents on that autumn day before I would walk into the *beis din* and ask for a *get*.

That day when I called my parents and they said "No" — they didn't fly across continents to stand by me when I needed them — was the day I *really* started to take responsibility for my own life, the day I felt a new sense of maturity enter my being when I surmised people are limited and that one cannot expect something from someone who doesn't want to give or who can't give.

That day I realized my history, my destiny; my life is mine and not my parents. And my parents' life, their destiny, their history, doesn't belong to me.

I realized only G-d can stand by me now for the rest of my life; because G-d is *always* available to help His daughter in need.

# 34

I t is late summer. In six weeks I will have to endure the two-year anniversary of my divorce. I wake up one morning and realize there are no more tasks on the rebbe's list, but something is bothering me. I realize I do not have peace with my parents; I feel they have not forgiven me for my mistake, for my marriage that ended after they paid for a wedding in Jerusalem, for the foolish time that has widened the gap in our relationship since the time of the *get*.

I decide to go to London to reconcile with my parents, particularly my father, who has practically ignored me since the divorce. I had been living in Israel for four years and even though my father and I have never had an amicable relationship, it had worsened since I left London.

On a sunny morning in August I took possession of a crazy idea — that if I could make peace with my father I would be blessed by G-d; that peace with my father would bring me the *brachah* I was praying for.

Once again, my memory faded and I forgot the fact that before you climb the highest mountain you should be prepared and seek support, take advice to ask if this is the right thing to do but I didn't this time — I was impetuous.

I called my mother and told her about my plan and made her promise she wouldn't tell Dad why I was coming back for a visit. I didn't tell anyone I was going, I just went.

The next week I knocked on the door of my parents' home in London.

"Who is it?" my father asked, on the intercom.

"It's me."

"Who's 'me'?" my father said.

"Your daughter!"

If I could have paid a million dollars for the first smile my father gave me when he opened the garden gate to their home, it wouldn't have been enough for what my father gave me in that instant; for a fleeting moment I felt his genuine joy and love and it was absolutely fantastic.

"So you came home for good," my father said.

"No, Dad, a visit."

A black cloud immediately descended on my father's now crumpled face as he turned inside, leaving the door open, and went back to his study to read the newspaper. Not the welcome I had hoped for.

The first day in London with my mother was busy and quite fun; we dashed here and there, doing lots of jolly things that made us laugh and smile and enjoy each other's company.

The next morning, bright and early, I was enjoying a fresh fruit breakfast with Mum over a good old chat (which, I knew, could not touch upon my being religious, divorced or impoverished — I had used my last savings to make this trip to London).

Ten minutes into our conversation, Dad popped his head into the kitchen.

"You mother says you want to talk to me. Come in now, please," said my father.

I looked at my mother and wanted to scream, "You didn't keep your word!" I wanted to do it in my own time, in my own way. I wanted to approach Dad with my olive branch of peace — when I was ready.

My mother's face read my message and paled; her hands covered her face in embarrassment. She wanted to say something — I believed she truly did — but she didn't. I felt sorry for her, but sorrier for myself. There was no way out; I grabbed my olive branch of peace and marched into the study.

Before I could sit down, my father closed the door and opened a dam of anger at me that I have never experienced before — a raging flow about everything to do with my life, my choices and my divorce. I was sure I had stepped into someone else's life, because, up until this moment, my volcanic father had given me no idea he was feeling all of these things under his veneer of masterful quietness and diplomacy.

About ten minutes into his attack on how I had wasted his money on a wedding that had embarrassed him, marrying a man that was an embarrassment to him, while my father was standing above my paralyzed form, the study door opened and my mother raised her voice to a level I never imagined existed in her repertoire of control management.

"Please stop this right now."

Mid-stream, my father immediately halted and retreated to his chair.

I looked at my parents and realized I had never done what they wanted. I had done everything wrong. All they wanted was a child who was happily married and financially secure; I was their disgrace — they were ashamed of me. I had made a lot of mistakes. They weren't interested in the good things I had done with my life; my errors were their misery.

I had pity on my parents, but I couldn't bring myself to say sorry. Their humiliation silenced me. I couldn't speak. I couldn't look at them. I was scared to say anything.

For the next six days I wandered the streets of London alone counting the hours until I could leave. My flight ticket was nontransferable. I had no money to purchase a new one. I had been out of touch with all of my London friends since I moved to Israel and they were out of town for the summer. It was a sad state of affairs; I endured each day with a heavy heart. I wandered through the London parks crying. I sat on park benches recounting my life, trying to figure out how I could have done things differently. I was a mess; I was desperate to get back to Jerusalem but had to wait patiently for each day to pass.

Finally, on the last day of my stay, I sat weary and teary-eyed in a bus shelter opposite an art museum I had just visited. The bus stop was crowded — it was hot, and London was bustling with tourists. I put my head on my knees, exhausted and resigned to the fact that I was a complete failure; I came to London to make peace and I had failed. How could I have been so stupid as to think I could change years of misunderstanding with my parents and make peace with a father with whom I have never been able to form a relationship? I felt miserable; I didn't know how I could carry on and how I would be blessed without peace in all areas of my life. I felt hopeless; I began to cry into my hands.

Just then someone bumped into me and startled me out of my stupor. I looked up. It was a girl wearing a sunny, bright yellow t-shirt. Sky blue letters danced across the happy color: Believe in Miracles.

I sat staring at these words. These words were created for me. Yes. The only way to carry on was to believe in miracles.

# 35

S ukkos was approaching signaling my annual visit to the Kotel with Rebbetzin Ruchoma Shain on the first day of Chol
Hamo'ed, a Sunday this year.

I had met Rebbetzin Shain at Harav Chaim Pinchas Scheinberg
*shlit"a*'s home during my first Chanukah in Jerusalem; since then I
had taken to visiting weekly to keep her company and get to know
her. She had become a published writer later in life; this was of
great interest to me, as was Rebbetzin Shain's wonderful character.
Every visit was a life lesson; every visit taught me how to conduct
myself as a thoughtful, caring person and I was grateful to my new
teacher, who taught by example.

The first day of Chol Hamo'ed Sukkos began like any other
beautiful day in Jerusalem — the golden sun rose and the birds of
Israel sang. I had a commitment to honor. I took a bus to collect
Rebbetzin Shain, who was waiting for me at her home in Mattersdorf, and then we took a taxi to the Kotel.

Rebbetzin Shain held my arm firmly as we walked towards
the crowded Kotel plaza; her petite under-five-feet frame leaning
into my five-feet-nine-inches towering posture. An atmosphere
of awe and joy was in the air. I was feeling particularly happy as
Sukkos is my favorite Yom Tov. I had dressed for the occasion
in a cream turtleneck and charcoal grey skirt. The burnt-orange
colored raincoat that my father had sent as a gift when my mother
visited, the year I had the terrible fall on the steps, added a splash
of color to my appearance. My *sheitel*, just washed and set for Yom
Tov, looked lovely.

Rebbetzin Shain, dressed in becoming shades of plum, stopped for a moment and pointed to the sky; a canopy of threatening dark rain clouds hung overhead.

"Hashem, please hold back the rain for us until we finish *davening*."

I smiled. I loved Rebbetzin Shain's relationship with G-d; she talked to Him like a Tatty and I felt a light pang of envy whenever I heard her speak like this; I wanted to feel this way and talk as effortlessly, too.

After we finished *davening* we made our way to the crowded bus stop. As we placed our feet on the steps of the bus, the clouds opened and buckets of rain drenched everyone waiting in line. I couldn't believe it but expected it — in a funny sort of way — Rebbetzin Shain's relationship with G-d was legendary.

A journey that usually takes twenty-five minutes took an hour and a quarter. While Rebbetzin Shain sat and I stood next to her, we chatted the whole way. Throughout our prolonged ride I was conscious of a lady in the seat in front of us; she was pregnant and had a small child with her. A tall handsome-looking man standing next to me was keeping the child entertained. He had a New York accent, sea-blue eyes and a calm demeanor. I found the scene endearing; the man's ways were pleasant to me and the child was so sweet. I sent a silent prayer to Hashem for such a husband and for such a situation.

After I saw Rebbetzin Shain settled in her comfortable chair at home with a cup of tea, I popped upstairs to see Rabbi Chaim Pinchas Scheinberg *shlit"a*, her brother-in-law and my rav.

"Can't you do anything for me? G-d can't hear me. I don't want to be divorced anymore. Please help me. Please *daven* for me today," I said.

The rav smiled and nodded.

"How much longer?" I asked him.

"A little more patience; it won't be much longer." He chuckled with a look on his face like he held a secret close to his heart.

I didn't understand. Frustrated, I traveled back home with my head resting on the wet pages of a *sefer* Tehillim.

That afternoon Rebbetzin Shain phoned me. She had a *shidduch* to tell me about: the person was the handsome man on the bus. He had been traveling back from a *shiur* on "Dating and *Shidduchim*" in the Old City by the Kotel. He had gotten off the bus a few stops before the stop where Rebbetzin Shain lived; he had gone to see his rav for *brachos* and to bemoan his single state. He had gotten back on the bus a few minutes before me on my return home after my conversation with Rabbi Scheinberg. He had watched me crying into my *siddur* and was perplexed; only a short while earlier he had seen me chatting happily with the rebbetzin, whom he recognized from a meeting in his mother's home for a charity event many years earlier.

The tall man on the bus was a year older than me, a *ben* Torah from a fine American family who had settled in Israel when he was eleven years old; his grandfather, Rabbi Nachum Tzvi Kornmehl *z"l*, a *dayan*, a Sanzer chassid from Vienna, had been the rav of Young Israel of Lawrence-Cedarhurst.

I made many thorough inquiries. So did a rabbi I asked to advise me objectively about the *shidduch* and his family. I learned that the man's father was a true *baal chessed* with a heart of gold; his mother a *yiras Shamayim*. He had five siblings, all living in Jerusalem and Bnei Brak. I learned that he had *smichah* from the Mirrer Yeshiva in New York, that he was also college educated, and that he worked with children as a special education rebbe.

The more I heard about him, the more at peace I felt about the idea of meeting him; I didn't want to rush into anything. I was adamant about taking things slowly.

Not for a moment did I think that I was a lesser person because I was divorced and that I was not a person of worth; on the contrary, after the counseling I had received from Rabbi Scheinberg and Rabbi Pliskin, my self-esteem was in a positive place even if I was apprehensive about trusting another husband. I felt the fate of my future laid in Hashem's hands. I prayed it would be in the merit of my efforts over the last two years, which were done *l'shem Shamayim* and my faith in G-d, that perhaps I would be blessed with a husband again.

Our first *shidduch* was Motza'ei Shabbos *Parshas Bereishis*, the first *parshah* in the Torah, heralding new beginnings.

# 36

I was determined not to make a mistake again. How would I know everything would be okay this time?

In a most self-effacing way, I broached many topics and issues with my *shidduch* to test out his opinion and feelings. I pressed for as much honesty and variety as possible in the meetings, so I could see this new man from numerous viewpoints.

We did something unconventional but important to both of us in the fourth week of the *shidduch*. I had dinner with his parents, to see if they were good people and if I liked them and if I felt they would accept me. Rabbi Zev Kotkes was such a warm, friendly person; upbeat with happy eyes and a big smile. He was so positive and welcoming that I felt at home with him immediately. Mrs. Kotkes doted on her son and husband; a real, live *eishes chayil* in full color.

A week later we had Shabbos with two families whom I had known for four years. My mother arrived beforehand mid-week and joined us; she visited, which was so helpful and welcome at this turning point in my life. She had lunch with his family and returned with a good report.

Shabbos was lovely and easygoing. My friends welcomed all three of us with wonderful hospitality, but I was nervous.

Rebbetzin Shain had phoned me just before Shabbos. "He's ready," she said. "Are you okay with this?"

"Yes," I said.

I was a little jumpy by *Havdalah*; he hadn't asked me yet.

"Let's go and see my rav, Rav Chaim Kanievsky," he suggested.

We traveled to Bnei Brak by bus, chatting harmoniously. Much to my confusion and disappointment, he avoided the topic of engagement.

While I waited under a lamppost, he went to talk to the rav, someone he had known since he was a teenager. He had asked him about all his *shidduchim*. He returned looking relieved; his eyes sparkled; his smile was beautiful. Still, he didn't say anything except to extend an invitation for me to return to the rav's home to meet Rebbetzin Kanievsky, who bestowed many *brachos* on me.

And still I was anxious; he still hadn't proposed.

We traveled home in silence; the darkness outside camouflaged our nervousness.

At two A.M., a taxi dropped me outside my apartment. He said goodnight; I rushed inside, weeping.

I sat by the clock and the phone. *If he doesn't call me within fifteen minutes, I will never see him again*, I said out loud to the silent apartment.

I waited — with G-d by my side — for a phone call.

Nine minutes later, enough time for him to get back to his apartment in Har Nof a few streets away, the phone rang.

"Leah, you'll be my wife, won't you?"

"Of course I will, silly; you could have asked me earlier."

We both sighed then laughed. It was such a funny conversation. It was such a big bridge to cross; trusting each other was all that mattered.

I was so happy; Mordechai Yisroel Kotkes seemed like a good person, a humble, dear person. Like me, he had been waiting a long time for a good person to come into his life; like me, he had been praying a long time for *brachah*.

The tall man on the bus and I became engaged — became *chassan* and *kallah* — Motza'ei Shabbos *Parshas Chayei Sarah*, and married the week Yaakov married Leah Imenu — *Parshas Vayetzei*, thirteen days later. This was the week of both of our birthdays. It seemed like a promising time to get married. Why wait, now that we had finally found each other?

Our wedding was a typical community-friendly *shtiebel* wedding. Rav Mayer Horowitz invited us to have the wedding banquet in his home. My close girlfriends cooked and coordinated the menu, and also decorated the house with flowers, ribbons and balloons.

Under a starry Jerusalem sky, and the sheltering birch tree outside the Horowitz home, my *chassan* and I stood under the *chuppah* with Harav Chaim Pinchas Scheinberg *shlit"a*, the Bostoner Rebbe *shlit"a* and Harav Tzvi Kushalefsky *shlit"a*.

I felt like the radiant sunshine under my thick white veil; no one could see my happiness, only G-d.

The street was full of hundreds of well-wishers and their children, many of whom had come especially to be with us, even though only eighty guests were joining us for the actual wedding meal.

I wore a dress of white silk with white pearls; Rav Scheinberg had told me to get the most beautiful dress in white and to enjoy my wedding.

An airport strike prevented my parents and brother from getting to the wedding on time. The Bostoner Rebbe's plane from New York was the last plane to come into Israel in the afternoon, giving him time to rest before he came to the *chuppah*.

Rebbetzin Ruchoma Shain couldn't be with us; this was sad

*My husband and me at the Kotel on our first wedding anniversary.*

for me. She had tripped over a telephone wire the day after she *redt* the *shidduch* and was hospitalized at the time. She sent a handwritten note and phoned during the evening, which brought fresh, happy tears to my eyes.

*Bli ayin hara*, Mordechai Yisroel I have been married for eleven years. *Bli ayin hara*, G-d has blessed us with a home in Jerusalem and four children. It's certainly a miracle to get married, but I only felt the beauty of the miracle when I got married a second time.

# 37

My mother made a turn about just before I got married. When I was dating my future husband she visited for a week and was gracious enough to honor my one request: to cover her head. Always a stylish dresser, Mum had got one of her dear friends to crochet matching berets to co-ordinate her outfits for the visit. I was so proud of her; she looked beautiful.

When we went to the Kotel to *daven* for *siyatta diShmaya* she borrowed my English *sefer* Tehillim and did her best to call on Hashem's mercy. I felt we were in this *shidduch* together. I loved Mum for being there for me when I really needed her.

When I was a little girl I never understood my mother, but I followed her like a lamb because she was all I had. Our family unit was four pillars, Dad, Mum, me and my brother. Grandma and my father's sister, who never married, were a "Sunday only appendix," as were my grandparents, Bubby and Zeide, and another aunt, my mother's sister, who never married either. A few other family members were inconsequential.

Mum was a devoted daughter; all week she industriously prepared for our jaunts down to Stamford Hill. I stood by the kitchen sink watching her *kashering* chickens for her mother's soup. I would help her pack up bags of clothes for her "special needs" sister, who lived "upstairs" in Bubby and Zeide's home. I heard her on the phone checking in to see all was well most days of the week.

At Dad's mother's apartment, Mum usually had her head in Grandma's freezer — three minutes after arrival — checking what

196

was needed for the next visit, confirming the shopping list with my aunt. While Grandma sat in her "widow's chair" and my aunt would serve tea and angel food cake, Mum would sit like a lady watching, waiting, ready for the ride to her parents and then home again.

Bubby was always standing in the kitchen before a soup pot nearly her size, which was petite. I don't recall tasting the soup, but the house smelled of it when we came in the narrow hallway of the two-up, two-down, a few streets away from Grandma's. Zeide's pinch on the right cheek throbbed of love for a whole week, as did the memory of his wide smile and jolly laugh that rocked his big teddy-bear-ish frame.

While the adults talked, my brother and I roamed around the garden and the lone apple tree, tiptoeing over the apple festooned floor. In season, the garden, which had a low fence and merged with the next on either side, smelled sweet, but when no one collected the apples, the rotten stench of decaying fruit was disgusting. This was where we waited until it was time to drive home.

Mum also loved our early morning Sunday walks at Kenwood House, a stately home in Hampstead Heath. The neatly cut grass, the huge blue and lilac hydrangeas, the rolling grassed hill that met the edge of a tree-edged lake with white swans. When I told Mum I dreamed of living in such a palace of a place, she didn't laugh. When I stood before the twenty-five-foot-high painting of the prancing Sandpiper horse in the art gallery in the house, the floor-to-ceiling-lined library, the regal, pretty floral bedrooms — all this was mine in my imagination — she listened and continued to take me to Kenwood House whenever I wanted to go. Even on weekdays, and even when I was older, because I loved this house and the gardens.

The drive through opulent Hampstead Garden suburb near

Kenwood to lowly Stamford Hill was an ugly contrast; I didn't
like taking leave of Kenwood, but I knew that we would always do
the right thing on Sundays. That was the way it has always been in
our family, due to Mum and Dad's steadfast rules of duty, which I
admired and respected — eventually.

If my brother and I were fortunate, my parents would also take
us each week to Golders Hill Park on the way home to feed the
ducks from the stone bridge over the lake, to watch the sheep and
goats frolic in the padlocked pasture, to admire the peacocks and
enjoy the petting zoo. They would wait patiently while we searched
for horse-chestnut conkers in the autumn among the thick weave
of gold, red, brown and orange leaves. It was a happy pastime. They
would also wait patiently while my brother and I went for donkey
rides around Hampstead Heath pond.

Mum and Dad were entwined in everything we did. Even when
Dad was overseas or at work, Mum was his partner in every way
and talked of him often to reassure us that Dad would be home
soon; managing the house, and us children, until he returned. All I
recall about my childhood was these Sundays and them keeping us
in a consistent routine on the days I was not at school. I knew what
to expect and it happened, as I anticipated, even the emotional
responses of my parents which were black and white, yes or no,
without variables. I didn't imagine Mum would express so much
sadness when I set off to settle in Eretz Yisrael. In the summer of
1993, her tormented face at the airport and her impassioned "I love
you" for the first time in my life was a surprise; her silence on the
phone a few days before my divorce was devastating.

So, it was a great joy to me when she also came to Israel two
months before I met my second husband; of course at the time we
had no idea this was to take place. She had chosen to join me on
a trip to pray for blessing and *siyatta diShmaya* at the *kivrei tzad-*

dikim, so that our prayers would merit special attention in G-d's eyes through the merits of the *tzaddikim*, and to see a *mekubal*, a holy man who it was said had the powers to see into the future with a great clarity, as I was desperate to know if I would re-marry. I was intrigued by Mum's enthusiasm to join me. Rebbetzin Shain's nephew was our guide; he took us up north in a mini bus with eight other participants including Rabbi Simchah Scheinberg *shlit"a*, my rav's son, and a *Chassidishe* couple on their first visit to Eretz Yisrael. Rav Simchah was thrilled to meet my mother — at last — after I had been a *bat bayit* in his parents' home for four years.

My mother was a real trouper; she picked up a *sefer* Tehillim, not her usual reading material, and she was ready to roll. I watched with awed curiosity as she prayed in her own special way at the *kevarim*. I was impressed with the way she handled her private meeting with the *mekubal*; when she returned her face shone with a light I have never seen before, her lips sealed, as the counsel was hers to keep.

On this day trip my mother made up for all the years I felt estranged from her; she was a role model, a spirited traveler, a kin-dred soul. She was the mother I had yearned for my whole life.

When I entered my fourth week of *shidduchim* with my future husband, my mother flew over for a week and stood on the side-lines in case I needed her. Her thoughtfulness made an impression at a time in my life when I wasn't sure how I was ever going to be a wife and mother at thirty-three years old.

Even though my mother came alone on these two visits just before I met my husband I knew deep down she was also an am-bassador for my father at all times and that he truly was with her in every way. I knew — I wanted to believe, I hoped with all my heart — that although he couldn't say it, he loved me really, truly and always had.

Recently, I read some of the hundreds of cards — each with a beautiful painting on the front cover — my mother has penned me since I settled in Israel which she always signed next to Dad's name also; all the words she has said to me in writing rather than face-to-face or on the phone. So many words that were comforting, helpful, understanding yet I never heard her voice them; their silent presence making an indelible impact on my growth as a Jew, a woman, her daughter.

I cherish these cards just as I cherish the words, just as I only recently came to appreciate the person I have only come to truly know by her silent acts of love, her words on paper and the gifts she sends in the mail. Her gifts of clothing as she has always been attentive to my presentation and apparel; the gift of her choice to be *mevater* on her own needs in London and put aside the money to send to me so I could have financial support when I really need it; the gift of her time while she penned those priceless words to me, so many thousands of miles away to a daughter who is raising her grandsons so far from her life, her reach, her heart that yearns to hug them, and love and kiss them. The pain this brings her is overridden by her desire that I be in a place where I can fulfill my potential: I know this now because recently she told me this on the phone but how I wish it had been in person or in writing, so I could re-read the words over and over again to know that her love is true.

I feel Mum epitomizes motherly love; the willingness to let go of something that is yours so that another can grow in his own way, even if you are not there to see it day-to-day. But when the letters and cards come, so does my mother's love, the love that I never felt as a youngster for some reason but always hoped with all my heart was there, the love that today exists because there is space for it where before there was no space for anything but Mum and Dad's own relationship.

*This is one of my favorite pictures of my mother; here she is having a special moment with one of our sons at the zoo in Jerusalem, the place we always visit when my parents come to see the children.*

# PART THREE

# *Jerusalem*

# 1

Marriage is like a garden; if you look after it, everything grows and blooms beautifully, but if you neglect it, things look undernourished and it is not a pleasant place.

When I was expecting our first child, I was busy from early morning to late at night teaching art and looking after our home. My husband was learning in *kollel* and was home very little in the day except for breezy breakfasts and relaxed dinners late at night.

In my eighth month of pregnancy — when I was starting to feel tired and a little overwhelmed balancing work, homemaking and the prospect of a new arrival — I asked a seminary girl to help me around the house in the afternoons and keep me company.

In her early twenties, Sonia was engaged to a boy in England and had come to Jerusalem to study while he was finishing up his law finals.

Sonia was starry-eyed about marriage. She talked non-stop about the type of home she and her *chassan* would have, the type of relationship they would have, the type of children they would have. She never stopped to ask me for my point of view on the topic of marriage. So I listened attentively as she weaved a pretty tapestry of idyllic bliss.

"And we put crystal glassware on the wedding list," she said. "How can a person have Shabbos without crystal?"

I didn't have the heart to tell her we managed very nicely without crystal in our first year of marriage; we had just celebrated our first anniversary when Sonia came to work for me.

At the end of a most elaborate and interesting ten-day mono-logue, Sonia finally asked me if I had any tips to share with her on the topic.

"Well, Sonia," I said. "I don't want to burst any fancy balloons but marriage is *avodas* Hashem. It's pretty hard work but it's worth it nonetheless."

She gave me a curious look.

"Leah, what are you talking about? I have never heard anyone talk about marriage this way."

"What I mean is marriage is hard work but it's worthwhile hard work; whatever effort you put in is returned to you in kind-ness — eventually. *Chessed* in marriage acts like a boomerang; whatever you put out comes back in the end," I said.

"I don't know what you mean. I wanted to know about recipes and things like that," she said.

"Sonia, before our wedding I asked my mother-in-law what my husband liked to eat. When we came to this apartment after the wedding my husband said he wanted a little snack and offered to make it himself. When he looked in the cupboards and found all the foods his mother told me he liked, he said, 'Oh, Leah, you see, now I know we are made for each other. We like all the same foods.'"

Sonia laughed for a long time.

"I love that story, Leah. Tell me more," she said.

"When you make the effort to give your husband what he needs and what he likes, everything will be good. My husband and I have dinner together every night: sweet potatoes and brown rice, his favorite, not mine, but he is not to know that. We talk about every-thing in his heart and he sees I am very interested because what is in his heart must be in my heart. This is how he sees it, and I don't disagree with him. I learn a lot about my husband this way; giving him what he needs has a boomerang effect. When I meet his needs he makes an effort to meet mine and day-to-day our marriage is growing in a positive way."

On Sonia's next visit, she insisted on serving me tea and asked if I could sit down for a little while.

"I'd be grateful to hear some more marriage advice," she said, taking out a new floral notebook.

We couldn't help laughing. From small acorns grow big trees; perhaps our conversations on the potential of *shanah rishonah* would help us both. Although we were years apart in age, in a short time I would only be a little way ahead of her on the marriage pathway, *baruch* Hashem.

"Once a month I really enjoy our Rosh Chodesh dinners. My husband doesn't really care for it. He takes me out because he knows it makes me feel special. We go to the same restaurant, the one where we once went on a *shidduch*. My husband laughs when I ask to sit in the same place we used to sit. 'I'm such a romantic,' he says. He loves that part of me. My husband is the most precious person in my life; his needs are the most important thing to me. When you tend to your marriage, the marriage will blossom. When challenges come your way, you will be able to work through them because you know how to talk to each other. You've learned to listen."

Sonia's eyes were bright; her cheeks flushed rosy pink, her hands clasped.

"I didn't know all this," she said.

"You'll learn on the 'job'. Now you have a few tips to put in your pocket," I said.

She hugged me tightly.

"Tips for life," she said.

"Some to start you off. I've only been married nearly a year. I'm sure there's tons more to know, but that should keep you busy for the time being," I said.

We both laughed.

On another occasion Sonia asked me who had taught me the best marriage tips before my *chuppah*. We were sitting at the kitchen table checking rice for any bugs.

"The Bostoner Rebbetzin Raichel Horowitz," I said, without thinking twice. "The Rebbetzin made marriage look simple, but she put all her effort into it."

I told Sonia I had been a *bat bayit* in the Rebbe *shlit"a* and rebbetzin's home for two years before I married.

"Tell me something special the rebbetzin told you," Sonia said, leaning forward attentively on her elbows.

"A few nights before I got married, the rebbetzin and I were huddled together at her dining-room table talking. The Rebbe had guests but the rebbetzin had asked me to come over late at night for a 'chat.' 'Leah, I want to tell you the secret of the success of my marriage,' she said. I looked into her kind face and knew what I was about to be given would be worth more than diamonds.

"'Forgive and forget, Leah,' she said. 'When you forgive and forget, you can begin again and move on. The rebbe and I don't dwell on things; we forgive each other after we have talked it through and then we forget about it. Tomorrow is a brand new day.'"

Sonia and I contemplated these words for a few moments.

I said, "Sonia, the rebbetzin gave me this gem of advice that I think was for me because funnily enough my husband is a master at forgiving and forgetting. Sometimes — more times than I like to admit — we get ourselves into a bit of a pickle. We don't give each other the support each of us needs, we demand too much of each other at times, or we don't take no for an answer. We try to have a kind, loving marriage, but sometimes we get tangled up in all sorts

*On my wedding day in December 1997 — Rebbetzin Raichel Horowitz a"h and me.*

of issues that are important to us — not knowing always how to communicate our wishes and needs clearly — and before we know it, we are pulling our marriage in opposite directions and we are not so happy with each other. The next day, my husband breezes in from morning *davening* with a song on his lips. He offers me a fantastic smile and a jolly greeting, acting as if yesterday was but a dream. I love my husband's ability to forgive and forget. If I try to talk to him about yesterday's woes he just smiles and says: 'That's history Leah. Let's move on.' And move on we do, *baruch* Hashem. Who knows where we would end up if it were up to me?"

Sonia and I had another good laugh and then I said, "G-d created man and woman as one soul in Heaven and then split that soul and sent them down into this world to find each other. There is no wisdom like the wisdom of G-d. When we marry we reconnect with the other half of our soul. The person G-d designed for us to help us achieve our *tikkun*, perfection, in this world is our *zivug*. Any wisdom we can pick up along the way, if implemented correctly, can only help us manage more effectively in all our relationships, including the one closest to us — our husbands."

I didn't talk to Sonia about my first marriage. I didn't tell her that sometimes a first marriage doesn't work out for the good and that it has to end in divorce; that G-d makes provisions for divorce because perhaps He wanted the couple to be married for a reason and only He knows the reason the marriage must be dissolved.

I didn't tell Sonia that when I married my first husband I knew that I would have to get divorced soon after, that three months after my marriage I received a *get*. It took me two years afterwards to refine myself through hard work and patience — to become a much more giving person, a person more ready to enter into a marriage relationship — before G-d gave me my second husband.

And the reason I didn't tell Sonia these things is because it is inappropriate to tell a young person, who has never been married, the trials and tribulations of marriage and what happens when things don't go according to plan and as a last resort the marriage must end.

# 2

My husband and I were blessed with our *bechor* in January 1999, a little over a year after our wedding day. By this time, my parents had visited once and spent considerable time poring over our wedding photos. They had graciously accepted my gentle, humble husband and finally things seemed to be on a peaceful, cordial footing.

On Shabbos, before we would welcome our community to a *shalom zachar* in our Brand Street home, my parents, brother and my in-laws joined us for a delicious meal our friends had prepared.

Before we sang *Shalom Aleichem*, my father-in-law invited me to stand before him; he blessed me with the traditional *brachah* for a girl — holding his hands high above my head. He did this every time we spent Shabbos with him and Ima at their apartment in the Shaarei Chessed neighborhood of Jerusalem.

Then my father-in-law, with his happy smile and dancing, sparkling eyes, asked my father to bless me and handed him a *siddur*; my father-in-law's custom was that of most religious parents — to bless their children on Friday night before the Shabbos meal. He didn't know that my father was not familiar with this custom.

When I was thirty-five years old my father blessed me for the first time on Shabbos *Kodesh*. It was a blessing I shall cherish my whole life.

# 3

*Early Summer 2000*

I am sitting in my Great-Uncle Dovid's Bat Yam apartment, half an hour away from Tel Aviv. He is my Zeide's brother. Zeide died when I was seventeen. I was in the hospice room when he passed away. My mother sat statue-like, in complete shock, while I stood holding my Zeide's hand, weeping. Death was familiar to me but that never stopped me from crying.

Great-Uncle Dovid is talking to my son, who is sitting in his stroller. Both are laughing; quite a pair already. I wish my Zeide

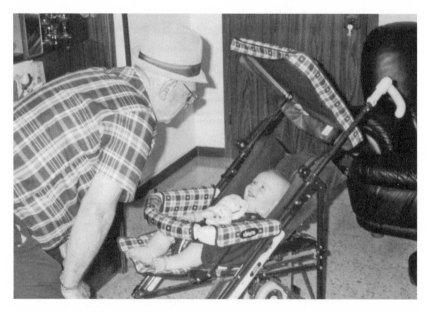

*Our bechor charming my Great-Uncle Dovid.*

was here to see this. I start to cry. Then I calm down. Zeide is here, he can see us from where he is. Why am I getting upset? My cousin is my interpreter. Dovid moved here after leaving Poland. Zeide went to England; Uncle Moshe to Australia. Uncle Dovid speaks Yiddish and Hebrew; I don't speak either language.

I ask Uncle Dovid about his parents, my great-grandparents. He walks off and returns with a framed photograph. My great-grandmother Chaya is wearing a *sheitel* and a serious face; my great grandfather Shalom looks the same, wearing a high black yarmulke.

Uncle Dovid talks about his childhood, about Warsaw, about running for his life. I am both teary-eyed and intrigued. Uncle Dovid is living history.

"Did my great-grandfather go to any Rebbes?" I ask.

"Yes," says Uncle Dovid, "the Rebbe of Gur; he went often to ask questions and ask for *brachos*."

I continue watching my son and my great-uncle in a dazed silence. Nobody notices, because the moment is so sweet; generations connect while a baby enchants a man in his eighties.

When I came to Israel I befriended a woman who taught me much about *tefillah* and *dveykus* to Hashem through prayer in your own words. The family were Gur chassidim. Her husband was the *gabbai* to the Pnei Menachem, the Gerrer Rebbe. I felt an affinity to Gur after seeing all the photographs of the Gerrer rebbes. For a few years I asked deeply personal and spiritual questions to the Gerrer Rebbe. In 1996, when the rebbe died I was devastated. By this time I had become close friends with another woman from Gerrer; we *davened* at the Gerrer shul once a month together on Shabbos, where I often listened to the Pnei Menachem's wife give a *shiur* to the women in the *ezras nashim* with my friend translating. After the Pnei Menachem passed away, I took to *davening* regularly at his *kever,* beside his father's *kever,* the Imrei Emes, a few minutes walk from Machane Yehudah Market.

While I watched my secular great-uncle, an Israeli citizen, play with my son, the son of a Torah scholar and rabbi, who has *yichus* back to Rashi and whose great-grandfather was a Sanzer rav in Vienna, I smile. Only one or two links in the chain of *Yiddishkeit* in my family history were broken by circumstances only my Zeide and my mother know, but, I, Leah Kotkes, have had the merit to repair the chain of *Yiddishkeit.* My son *baruch* Hashem will grow up in a home of Torah and *mitzvos* and will have opportunities that I did not have.

If my Zeide had not left Poland to avoid conscription he may not have survived World War I. If he would have survived, it is likely he would have not survived World War II. If he would have survived, perhaps my mother and I would have grown up in Poland. "Perhaps," "if" — are past. This is the future. I cannot change my grandfather's or my mother's choices. I can only write my own

*My great-grandparents Shalom and Chaya Bloomberg.*

life story. Free choice changes destinies. I am in charge of my own choices now. I can affect my future and that of my children's with my free will.

I say goodbye to Great-Uncle Dovid and walk to the bus stop. The air is humid, the sky a fantastic blue. I am in Eretz Yisrael pushing my son in a stroller along the streets of a land I love with all my heart. Soon I will be back in Jerusalem with my husband who is now in the *beis medrash* learning Torah.

*Hodu laHashem ki tov, ki l'olam chasdo*; thank Hashem for He is good, for His kindness is everlasting.

# 4

My parents fell in love with their first grandchild; they couldn't stop holding him and stroking his face and talking to him sweetly.

I prayed our son would bring my parents and me together on a more regular basis. I was very happy when they came to Israel to celebrate his first birthday with us. Dressed in a jolly red birthday outfit and holding a smiley yellow balloon, my endearing little son managed to woo my father to the carpet where they built a Lego tower together. The birthday boy established an immediate fondness for the giant brown bear with the burgundy bow-tie my father chose as a gift.

Two months after our second child was born we moved to a new home my father-in-law and my father bought for us. This gift was truly something special to us, an event that allowed me to finally thank my father for his benevolence from as far back as I can remember.

My father didn't totally abandon me after I left London; he did occasionally send money through

*It brought me much joy to see my father holding our son; my father was enchanted by him and I was enchanted by my father's love for his first grandchild.*

my mother for me, but I didn't hear more than a "Hello, here's your mother" on my weekly phone calls to Mum. Sadly, I never saw his handwriting in a card or in a letter, just Mum's. This pained me very much. Thinking about it now, it seems to me that Dad disliked that I was not becoming the daughter he had hoped for. When Dad and my father-in-law decided to take care of our mortgage I was so grateful and surprised; I often heard people saying "a parents' love conquers everything." Now I knew what that meant firsthand.

The move to our new home was an exhausting undertaking for me. My second son was two months old, I had a toddler at my skirt and there was much to do to organize my family into the new apartment. We were delighted with the increased space, the pine forest view and the little garden complete with rose bushes.

Six weeks later I started to worry that something was seriously wrong with me; I felt low, had trouble sleeping and cried a lot.

I thought perhaps I was experiencing post-partum depression but decided that this change in my personality was due to having two children a year apart, the house move and now being a little distant from familiar friends. Also I had isolated myself; I had not been to a *shiur* or even on a walk in months. I wasn't in the company of anyone, including children from the community, as I had closed the Art Club before my second son was born. Under-stimulated, in the midst of, albeit happy, mundane motherly and homemaking duties, I was feeling down and depressed.

A blood test showed low iron, so I did what I had to do to up the count, but my mood remained down. I was convinced I should have been feeling fantastic after moving to a new home and having a new baby but I wasn't; somehow a flow of negative energy had entered my being. I woke up every day feeling like the whole world was on my shoulders and I was totally alone. This was partly true — my husband was out all day, teaching every the morning in a yeshivah and learning in a *kollel* in the afternoon and early evening — and I had two children to look after and a home to manage. Every small thing seemed too much for me.

"You need to relax more," said my husband.

"I can't sit down for a moment. There's always so much to do and most times I just don't want to do it," I said.

"I'll help where I can but is there something else you're feeling that you aren't telling me?" he said.

"Yes, I feel so low lately. Like everything I do is never good enough. I just want to stop and slow down and feel good about what's going on in our life," I said.

"You need something to boost your self-confidence," said my husband.

"I'm out of ideas," I said.

"I don't have any either, but I'm sure Hashem will tell us what to do next. Wait and see," he said.

At the, time we were sitting on our new sofa — a wedding gift from my brother — when suddenly, the phone rang.

We looked at each other and laughed. Perhaps the answer was at the end of the phone line. Funnily enough it was.

Rabbi Yisroel Roll, a friend of Rabbi Simon and one of my spiritual mentors from London, had moved back to Baltimore, Maryland in America. He was in Jerusalem for a week. He called to invite us to a two-hour *shiur* he was giving to launch his new 12-Steps-to-Self-Esteem twelve-week self-help program that he had created in partnership with Rabbi Avraham Twerski, M.D.

My husband and I went along to the separate-seating *shiur*. Rabbi Roll presented a program that sounded so fresh and interesting. Most of the how-to ideas I had never heard before; all of them were very inspiring and seemed attainable. Excited, I asked Rabbi

Roll if I could host a program for women in my home. He readily agreed to train me via e-mail, and we started our correspondence a week later.

Two months later, I felt prepared and ready to advertise the program in our local community newsletter. Three weeks after that, I welcomed thirty-six women to our apartment for my first twelve-week program. This gave me an opportunity to give something of value to Jewish women while helping me to rebuild my self-confidence after the life-changing events of the last four years.

## Because I was Created by G-d

I take my eldest son to *cheder* every morning. The walk home is a delight: a downhill path with the Jerusalem Forest to my right and rolling forested hills that recede into a valley and touch the horizon straight ahead.

Once upon a time, before my first child was born, this was a familiar walking route. At 5:30 A.M. the air was different; if you have ever inhaled early morning air you know what I mean.

Today, halfway through my descent at 8:30 A.M. an empty bench beckoned me. While my eyes scanned the view around me, I decided this would be an excellent place to do an exercise from the 12 Steps-to-Self-Esteem Program.

The previous night, we had been discussing Step 7, which begins with the affirmation; *I am entitled to regard myself with value and worth because I was created by G-d; therefore, I have intrinsic value and worth just by being, not by doing or accomplishing.* The program doesn't follow the steps in order: Step 7 was an antidote to Step 1, *I admit that I have a low regard for myself, do not value myself and do not think I have much to offer others.*

After I found a point of focus in the landscape, I closed my eyes. The silent scene was conducive for the exercise. *Relax. Relax the different areas of your body starting with your feet and work your way up toward your head. Relax the muscles in each section. Now dig deep within your mind and psyche and find the part of you, which is warm, positive, gentle, compassionate and good. This is your spiritual center. It is your soul, your* neshamah. *You have put your finger on the G-d given Life Force within you. Stay with the feeling for two or three minutes.*

As I began to let go and allowed myself to enjoy this opportunity of thinking about my soul, a peaceful, weightless feeling embraced me that was so pleasant it made me smile.

*Now, draw an imaginary line from your spiritual center and allow it to extend from inside you and go beyond you into outer space. Let it keep stretching outward toward infinity and let it reach up to its source, the source of the warm and positive feeling. You are now getting in touch with your Creator; the source of your positive Life Energy. You are now getting in touch with the Divine. Just as the sun warms the earth allow the Source of the warm feeling to fill you with more warmth and good feeling.*

For a period of time, in my mind's eye I saw myself standing in space that felt familiar and beautiful, spacious and radiant. I felt safe, protected and loved. I felt so sweet inside, so happy, so relieved. I felt this must be the place I can feel the closest to *Hakadosh Baruch Hu* right now. I recollect thinking at one point, He is there just for me, isn't that wonderful? I liked this place. I was grateful it exists and it is mine.

Hoot! Hoot! A car horn blared.

"Can I take you somewhere?" said Sarah, trying to compete with a crescendo of classical music inside her car. "Are you okay, Leah? You look a strange sight sitting there with your eyes closed."

It was true. I felt vacant and calm while I sat on the wooden bench perched on a swooping hill in our community. By the look on Sarah's face, it was obvious she was waiting for some sort of explanation.

"I'm fine, Sarah. Really, I am. Thanks for the offer, though," I said.

"Okay, see you another time," she said with a swish of a hand-wave, and zoomed off up the hill.

*How ironic*, I thought, as I saw her car fumes disintegrate into the atmosphere. There I was, traveling to a spiritually secure place, and in the midst of "being present," in the quiet of my mind in union with G-d, someone stops to offer me a "physical" ride somewhere.

The comparison amused me; I looked up into the sky and offered a nod up to the Heavens; it all seemed like another perfect example of *hashgachah pratis*; I had just traveled to the only place I wanted to be right now in my life, a place unreachable by car.

The exercise taught me that when I feel close to G-d there is no reason to feel negative feelings about myself and my life; if I do, perhaps it's a sign for me to look more closely at the link that connects me to my Creator. I know He wants to send down to me a flow of blessings and positive energy always.

That day on the bench I felt sure Hashem loves me unconditionally; He accepts me just the way I am at all times; whether I am juggling the roles and responsibilities of my life or sitting on a bench thinking about nothing except how grateful I am to be in G-d's world and the recipient of G-d's goodness.

# 5

One day, a little before Chanukah 2000 arrived — when my two children were nearly two years old and seven months respectively — I woke up feeling a bit fuzzy; like everything in my life was merging together.

What was happening here? I thought about this all day until I decided that I wasn't finding a place for myself in my life. I was a wife, mother, homemaker, and facilitator to women on the self-esteem programs.

Where was my space? Where was "I" in the picture of my life?

I wrote a poem after a friend loaned me a book about redefining one's personal boundaries. The self-help book introduced me to a lot of new ideas and ways to place new boundaries in my life but this poem I wrote helped me more. It helped release a lot of pent up frustration and affirmed what I was feeling and ultimately, helped me to make changes.

Writing is a wise old friend. I always gain from what I pen in my journal.

### Space

I didn't understand the importance of defining
   and guarding one's boundaries
— until recently
I didn't realize how vital boundaries were.
All my life I just existed in someone else's space,
someone else's place until

I felt uncomfortable, threatened or simply bored,
    then I moved on.
This is not life.
That is why my life was difficult,
sad and lonely and unproductive.

Being married and being a wife
gives me a border.
A role, a defined name.

Is a border a name?
A role?
A responsibility?
A job?
Or is it a fence?

Being a mother gives me a border
A role
A defined job
Being a person...
Being a writer...
Being...
Are borders being?
Do I have many borders or just one?
What do borders mean?

I think it means
This is me.
This is my body, my voice
This is my mind,

my place to think and dream

This is my heart,

a treasure chest for my emotions.

This is my soul,

the deepest, most precious part of me.

Behind this boundary

is what is important to me.

My values,

morals

my spiritual preciousness,

my intellectual perspective.

Please accept and respect me;

I am a person

Please accept and respect my feelings,

my ideas,

my contribution,

my place in the world.


Don't deny my boundaries

Don't infringe on my borders and hurt me

Don't ignore my boundaries and push me by as if
  I were invisible.

Stop.

Listen to me.

Look at me.

Hear me.

Acknowledge me.

I am someone

I am me

I count
G-d created me
My boundaries define me
My boundaries show the world I exist,
I have a reason to be here
This is my mark
That defines
My place
My space
To be me
And give to the world
The way I know how.

How much transition and trauma can a person go through before they break? Perhaps I wasn't being kind enough with myself. Perhaps I wasn't taking care of myself well enough or being patient enough with the chapters of my life that were unfolding under Hashem's watchful gaze. I had moved to a new country, transformed my identity, adopted a new name, taken on a new way of life, married, divorced, struggled with the ordeal of being single again and then remarried and now I was a mother responsible for two children and a home and I had recently taken on a new job as a self-esteem counselor. But had I put up firm enough boundaries between these roles so I could grow at a healthy pace? Did I leave a big enough space for self-care as I grew upwards towards G-d's expectations of me?

Take it easy, Leah, I coached myself. Go with the flow. Redefine and appreciate your boundaries.

Surely every human being deserves respect from others simply because of basic respect and dignity. Surely boundaries in all areas of life are a base-line need and requirement for healthy living?

Analyzing and redefining my personal boundaries was painful; it brought up all sorts of issues from my childhood and first marriage. Still, I was so happy I made the time to work through some of my boundary issues and feelings. It helped me move into a more conscious position; I started to learn how to be available to others while making space for self-care, without feeling confused, resentful or guilty for saying, "No, I am sorry I cannot do that today or anymore," or the courage and confidence to simply say, "No" — period.

# 6

As is my custom, I went with my husband to see Harav Chaim Pinchas Scheinberg *shlit"a* with our two children on the third day of Chanukah. At this time of year, the season of miracles in the Jewish calendar, I was now relieved to recall my first visit in 1993 when I was single. Now it was the year 2000; how my life had changed for the good since then.

After the rav had given the children *brachos*, he asked my husband to take the children into the kitchen to see the rebbetzin for a cup of apple juice and some Bamba; the rav said he wanted to talk to me privately.

"Is there something the matter? When you arrived, I noticed you seem a bit down," said the rav.

"I don't feel so good. I feel so low. I've got no energy," I said.

Then I told the rav about the iron deficiency and what I was doing about it and the work I'd been doing on redefining my boundaries and my priority list at home.

"Good," he said, "But you also need to go out a few times a week. Perhaps go for a swim once a week and go to a *shiur* or see a friend. It's important to get out of the house and do something for yourself when you have small children. You'll come home rejuvenated."

"You're right. I hardly do anything for myself anymore. Thank you for the encouragement." I said.

227

"There is something else I would like you to do," the rav said.

I perked up when Rabbi Scheinberg said this — he had never spoken to me this way.

"I want you to write a book. I want you to tell women your story. I feel sure it will inspire them and help someone along the way."

I couldn't believe it; I had never told the rav about my childhood dream to be a writer.

"In fact, I want you to write the first chapter tonight and phone me when it's done," he continued.

As the time to light Chanukah *licht* drew closer, we bid the rav and rebbetzin goodbye. I was grinning all the way home in the taxi; my *rav* had come up with the excellent solution to my low mood.

At 11:40 P.M. I put down my pen.

"Do you think the rav really meant it?" I said to my husband. He nodded.

"Let me read you what I wrote," I said.

My husband's eyes were wet by the time I stopped reading. His face had taken on an endearing glow. He urged me to make the call and stood next to me while I dialed.

The rav picked up the phone.

"Rav? It's me, Leah," I said.

"Did you finish the first chapter?" he said.

"Yes."

"Well done! Keep going and have *hatzlachah*," my rav said.

The book you are holding in your hands is the same book I started in December 2000. The rav constantly prodded me on — every time I saw him since our conversation, which has probably been over a hundred times, he would ask me, "How is the book coming along?"

So the obvious question is, why did it take me just over nine years to write it? Surely if my rav said that I should write a book, and I follow *daas* Torah, I should have done it straightaway.

One of the reasons this book was completed at a much slower pace than I would have liked, is because it took me much longer than I thought to muster up the courage to take on the task of writing a full-length book, and when I did, everything went relatively smoothly, *bli ayin hara*.

# 7

After our Chanukah visit to Rav Scheinberg *shlit"a*, the next eight months flew by.

Our children's growth and progress thrilled my husband and me as we rejoiced in the gift of parenthood G-d had kindly given us from His bounty.

Writing time for the book ebbed and flowed like a meandering stream through the days of my busy life. When I made time to write, I felt wonderful and I advanced in the manuscript. When I thought about writing when I couldn't write, because I was looking after our two children in-between keeping house and spending quality time with my husband, I resigned myself to the fact that it was going to be a very long time before I had a published book in my hand.

Serving G-d and taking good care of my family had to come first. I knew my writing would always be way down the priority list. Without extra money for home-help or any extended family available to help me with the children, I would have to do what I could, when I could.

As the heat of the early summer made its way into our lives, heralding a stretch of lazy days in the park and picnics with the children, we received the special news that I was expecting our third child. We kept our news private, as is our custom, and I prayed each day for a healthy, beautiful child with true *kavanah* in my heart.

Three months later I woke from an afternoon nap with excruciating pains. The next thing I knew, I was speeding along in a taxi curled up like a ball on the back seat, sobbing in between spasms of agony.

On August 15, 2001 — the eighth anniversary of my arrival in Israel — I had a miscarriage.

For two days I lay in the hospital bed in a trance-like state, my mind whizzing through all the precious moments in my life when G-d had been kind to me. I so desperately wanted to find the good in what was happening now in this sad situation, because it had to be somewhere, as this was also part of G-d's plan.

I was stunned — I couldn't believe what had happened. How could G-d give and then take? How could He give me a child and then take the child back again?

For weeks after my return home from the hospital, I hardly spoke. Across my face passed wisps of confusion and anguish, like threatening rain clouds being pushed by the wind. I tried so hard to hold back the tears, to believe everything G-d does is for the best — but most days I just couldn't wing it.

The festive holiday of Sukkos was fast approaching. Inspired by my husband's optimistic mood — he is an advocate of positive energy overriding the negative — we invited my parents-in-law to our sukkah. The invitation forced me to get myself together to prepare a lovely meal in honor of Chol Hamo'ed.

"Leah, don't be sad," said my father-in-law.

"I'm sorry, Abba. I can't help it. I really wanted another child — the whole thing was such a shock to me."

"Don't worry, Leah. Hashem won't forget you; He's going to collect your tears and give you something very precious very soon. I'm sure of it."

"Amen," I said, blessing my beloved father-in-law's kind and considerate words that filled me with hope.

# 8

Over the next three and half weeks my father-in-law kept up his daily, "Good morning, Leah. How are you?" phone calls. He had been calling me like this throughout my four years of marriage, but now he was adding much-appreciated advice and words of inspiration. He suddenly took to popping in a few times a week to sit with the children and me in the garden as well as on his regular weekday night with Ima for dinner. As he watched the children, he would tell me about his own childhood, reflect on his life and give me points of inspiration on how to raise his grandchildren.

One day he stood in the hallway, holding a cassette tape in his hands.

"Leah, I can't stay long today," he said. "I have a meeting in Har Nof." As usual, Abba was dressed like a true gentleman and his face was radiant with goodwill.

"Leah, I know *Parshas Lech Lecha* is your favorite *parshah*, too. Take this tape and listen to it and tell me what you think."

He handed me a *shiur* by his beloved Rebbe, Rav Yosef Dov Soloveitchik of Yeshiva University.

"You know Leah, this *parshah* taught me so much about life," said Abba.

I looked at my father-in-law; I couldn't wait to hear what message he was sending me via this *shiur*.

"Leah, you must not worry about anything in life. You're never alone. Hashem will always be with you."

I had to hold back the tears; this is the way I had been thinking since I was a girl. How odd Abba should say the same exact words to me.

"*Hakadosh Baruch Hu* walked with Avraham Avinu, Leah. He will always walk with you; you will never be alone or lonely."

He then looked at me most intently and said goodbye.

My in-laws joined us for a meal once a week in our home; Abba never came alone. In the month of November in the year 2001 he came about eight times, each time sharing an unforgettable thought of this kind.

# 9

The shrill ringing of the phone pierced through our afternoon naps. We had all gone to bed unusually late the night before. Two days ago, my parents had made a spontaneous five-day visit from London to see the children. We were due to meet them at the hotel for an early dinner.

I took the phone call a little groggily; more sleep would have been wonderful.

"Leah, where have you and Mordechai been?" yelled by brother-in-law. "I've been trying to reach you for an hour. Abba had a heart attack at 3 o'clock this afternoon. We're all here with him at Sha'arei Tzedek Hospital in Cardiology Intensive Care."

An image of my father-in-law standing on my front doorstep holding a tape he had brought for me to listen to just last week popped into my mind; then I ran to wake my husband.

We left our two children with a neighbor as we flew like angels with prayers on our lips to Abba's bedside. I can see my husband and me racing through the corridors of Cardiology. I felt like my heart would explode if I ran any faster.

The scene that greeted us was horrific. I knew when I saw Abba that it was only a matter of time — I had seen death coming before — purple-black bags of urine, jittery, dancing red lines on a respirator monitor, puffy face and lips, and a sheen of angelic powder hovering over the one you love.

My husband's family was sitting on chairs facing the bed saying

Tehillim — five siblings and four spouses trying to concentrate on prayer, their heads dipped into their books, my mother-in-law statue-like beside the bed guard.

"Abba!" I screamed, instantly taking in the vital signs.

"Abba, it's Leah and Mordechai. We're here now. We love you, Abba. You have to fight this, Abba, with everything you've got."

I was hushed immediately; for the next fifteen minutes the twelve of us respectfully said Tehillim in silence.

I prayed from a place in my heart that opened for me like a treasure chest. In no time at all my *sefer* Tehillim was drenched; my body shaking with the prospect of what was to come.

I had been in this place before — with my beloved Zeide when I was seventeen years old — and the signs were too familiar to me. Yet the Jewish tradition lives with the belief that anything is possible, that G-d can nullify a bad decree and create a miracle in the blink of an eye.

When a few family members excused themselves, I sprang forward and closed the door, then ran to the head of the bed; I knew from the end-of-life experience with my Zeide and all the books I read on the topic that a person can hear what is going on, even if they seem comatose. My own grandfather had woken for a brief spell, told me so, and then slipped into eternity.

"Abba, we're all here and we want to tell you how much we love you," I said. "Come," I said to some of my siblings-in-law, "come here and tell Abba how much you love him."

Within a second, everyone was by the bed and each person said a few words in between their wailing. The room took on a warm glow and the feeling of unity was beautiful, even though the silence was replaced with pitiful cries.

For the next five minutes, my husband and I learned from the *Chumash* he had brought along and spoke about the *parshah*.

We talked about all the shared moments in our life with Abba. We spoke quickly in animated voices, and then everyone else spoke, and our love for Abba permeated the room until there was not a speck of space that was not filled with our gratitude to Abba for our lives, our marriages and our children.

When we finished talking, I moved my face very close to Abba.

"Abba, we love you so much. Please, Abba, don't leave us now. We all need you, I need you, my children need you."

We were silent, waiting, hoping for him to say something — wishing him to life. Each person was either holding one of Abba's hands or touching his body softly.

And then something remarkable happened. Abba turned his head to where my husband and I were standing and opened his eyes — and I believe, perhaps because I wanted to and perhaps because I was absolutely sure — I saw Abba's soul in his eyes, a bright, beautiful shining light that I had never seen before in the eyes of anyone I had ever met. The moment of truth was fleeting but we experienced it and it shook us all to the core.

A few seconds later the head nurse ran into the room.

"What's going on here?" she demanded. "The machines are jumping like crazy — your father's fighting this thing. It's extraordinary."

We stared at her as she scanned Abba's body for something to explain his momentary reflex.

When the other members of the family returned, everyone's hands dropped from their place. I stepped back from the bed and felt scared; how were we going to win this battle now? How were we going to come out of this not feeling guilty and annoyed because we couldn't say what was in our hearts to the beloved man lying so close to us?

In the evening, only my mother-in-law and two family members remained.

An hour before we went to sleep, my husband and I sat with my emotionally drained parents; they couldn't believe the turn of events.

"Let us know what is going on in the morning," said my father. He was standing at the front door while my mother was putting on her coat.

"We all need to pray," I said.

The next day my neighbors watched the children again. The whole family sat with Abba, deep in prayer.

At four o'clock I left the hospital for an hour with my two sisters-in-law. I had made up for my parents to see the children. as I rushed home I berated myself that I had agreed to this plan under the circumstances; all I wanted to do was to be by Abba's bedside, talking to him and praying.

While my children were enjoying their grandparents' company the phone rang. It was 4:45 P.M. I shrieked when my husband told me Abba had just died.

I wanted to reach up to Heaven and pull my father-in-law back down to Earth; I felt as though G-d had made a mistake, *chas v'shalom*. We all needed Abba. I needed his love for the rest of my life, to be the best wife I could be to his son and to give me strength to raise his grandchildren.

My parents, too distraught to deal with the situation, left for their hotel within five minutes of the tragic phone call. I had to find a friend to watch the children before I could go back to the hospital to say goodbye to Abba.

I walked tentatively into the hospital room; even though I was eager to say my farewell, all of the sudden, I was overwhelmed by the prospect.

Abba was clothed in a black plastic body bag. The nurse pulled the zipper to expose Abba's face; death looked me straight in the eyes and it was terrifying.

*This is going to be me one day. Oh my G-d, I don't want to die. Oh my G-d, Abba wake up, we need you, I need you.*

Words poured out of me as fast as my gushing tears. *No, no, no, this is not what I want, G-d. No, this is a mistake. Abba, wake up. Abba, come back to us.*

Three hours later I took a pair of scissors from the director of the *chevra kaddisha*. I had asked to be the one to cut the cloth so I could also feel the incision in my heart.

In the chilly stone room of the funeral parlor I stood before each sister-in-law and did what the *halachah* tells you to do to the clothes of a mourner.

Then I sidestepped. Standing before my mother-in-law, I looked into the eyes of a widow. I could feel the witnesses watching me, all those who had crowded around us.

I lifted the scissors to the fabric of her shirt, all the time our eyes locked, never blinking, never detaching from the reality of the moment. Abba's body was beside us on the floor, wrapped in a shroud.

I cut the cloth — slowly and carefully — and I felt "someone" cutting the cloth of my life, making it smaller while they whispered in my ears, *Don't waste a moment of it, Leah. It moves so fast and it ends so quickly.*

# 10

I became unrecognizable after my father-in-law died; I became manic about not wasting time. I became more focused, more determined, more ready to forego anything and everything that got in the way of doing what I needed to do.

How much time did I have left? I begged Hashem for as much time as I needed to do what He wanted me to do with the life and gifts He gave me. I prayed for life and worried about how many years, months, days, minutes, seconds I had left.

I cleaned the house from top to bottom. I discarded what we didn't need or use. I updated all our household business. I made peace with everyone, just in case there may have been something I said sometime, anytime, that upset someone.

I was frantic; I wanted things to be just so in case something happened to me. I wouldn't go on a bus in case, G-d forbid, a terrorist would board. I only took taxis when I had to. I was anxious, I was nervous. I kept asking G-d and then Abba *z"l*, What do you want me to do with my time?

When I passed black and white *"Baruch Dayan Emes* — G-d is the true Judge" Jewish community death notices, I would stare at the words and shudder.

After a good few months I told myself I was being ridiculous, that G-d will decide when it's my time, but I still had to decide how to use my time — without wasting a moment.

Abba was very encouraging when I told him Rabbi Scheinberg's suggestion to write a book; in fact, whenever I spoke with Abba, he would ask me how I was progressing. This always prompted me to think of how blessed I was to have such a caring mentor in my life.

Thirty days after Abba's *petirah*, I was asked to give the opening speech at a charity fundraising event for mothers and daughters at which Rebbetzin Shain was the keynote speaker. The evening's theme was *simchas hachaim*, the joy of life.

I was so happy to tell the three hundred attendees a little about the story of Abba's life — he was an *eved* Hashem who exuded *simchas hachaim,* a joy for life. He helped finance *yeshivos*, he helped many *tzedakah* organizations, he loved to assist others. He had a heart of gold and a smile that would light up a room and the soul of every person.

At the end of the evening a *Chassidishe* woman came up to me.

"I must compliment you on your speech. Did you write it yourself?" she asked.

"Yes, I did. I like to write."

"Would you like to write for us?" she asked.

"That sounds interesting. Who are you?"

The woman was an editor at *Hamodia* Magazine, a supplement of a leading Torah newspaper.

I was thrilled with the idea; I could not believe such an offer was coming my way on such a night.

My first interview column called, "Pillars of Strength," profiled rebbetzins and appeared in *Hamodia* Magazine in May 2002, five months after Abba left this world and five months before a child would be named in his memory.

When I think of Abba, I get very emotional, my eyes usually cloud over and tears well up — I loved him because I felt his love for me. But he has not gone far from my life. On the contrary, every time I need to, I think of Abba and call up his face. I see his twinkling eyes, and kind smile, and I carry on doing the best with the resources G-d gave me, knowing Abba can see me. I hope he is proud of my efforts.

# 11

I have learned a lot from reading books and listening to people talk about their lives. Many have told me that it says in the Torah when something bad happens to us it is G-d's way of talking to us; when big things happen that we don't understand, G-d is saying: I tried to tell you quietly and because you didn't listen, I had to shout.

When I was six months pregnant with our third child, who is named after my father-in-law, we were invited to have the Pesach *seder* with my husband's brother in Ramat Bet Shemesh. My husband wanted to be with one of his brothers for Yom Tov. Being with his family for this first Yom Tov since Abba's parting was so very important to him.

"It will make Abba happy," he said, trying to keep up a brave face. My husband was very close to his father; the loss was very great in his life.

We had a lovely Yom Tov, but all the time I was anxious; I had a peculiar feeling that our home wasn't safe.

Just as we were about to drive away from Ramat Bet Shemesh my brother-in-law whispered something into my husband's ear; he was sitting in the front seat of the taxi. My husband flinched and then strengthened himself. When I asked my husband what was wrong, he didn't answer.

"We had a burglary, didn't we?" I said.

He tipped his head slightly. We rode home in silence.

The front door was latched from inside so we couldn't get in.

Our neighbors kindly watched our two sleepy children while my husband climbed into the house through the windows in our living room, which are guarded by metal doors that were now thrown open.

The apartment was neat and clean, just as we had left it. Everything was in its place in the living room, *baruch* Hashem — the *tefillin*, the Shabbos *licht*, and every other item of value in our lives.

The computer on my desk in the study was gone — along with the chapters of my new book that I had not backed up. Our bedroom was turned upside down; all my clothes, shoes, jewelry, and bed linen were gone. Nothing else had been taken.

G-d was upset with me.

I was silenced. I was very hurt. Couldn't G-d have spoken to me more kindly? On the other hand, thank G-d, we weren't home, no one was hurt, the rest of the house was in order, but a part of me had been taken away. Why?

When I phoned Rabbi Scheinberg to tell him about the robbery, he said, "You will see miracles by the end of this week."

I wanted to believe him, but why should G-d grant me miracles when He had just taken everything away?

The next day my sister-in-law brought over a selection of nearly new maternity clothes as a gift. Four days later, a package arrived from the US with new bed linen from my husband's cousin selected to match our peach and mint green bedroom decor.

The next day, Erev Shabbos, an hour and a half before candle-lighting there was a knock at our door. It was our neighbor, Yosef.

"I sat down and thought what I would feel like if someone took my computer," said Yosef. "I felt pretty lousy about the idea, so I brought you a spare one from my storage room."

In a box by his feet was the computer. He was holding the screen and keyboard in his hands.

I looked at Yosef and blinked.

"Is this really happening?" I asked.

"Yes," said Yosef. "Can I come in and set it up for you?"

I stood to one side and he walked in laughing; he was so happy to be helping us and I laughed also. I was so happy there was something called a miracle.

I called Rabbi Scheinberg when our neighbor had left to tell him what had happened to me in the last few days. He laughed and said he was pleased to hear the good news and wished me a good Shabbos.

I had a very good Shabbos. I had been graced with G-d's favor and now I had to do serious *teshuvah*; G-d had given something to me — He had shown me He had not abandoned me.

Now it was my turn.

I made an arrangement with G-d the day our neighbor brought his computer — the last miracle of the week that was causing my eyes to shine. I committed myself to writing for Klal Yisrael as my thank-you gift, and that is what I have been doing ever since.

After the robbery, I portrayed the epitome of gratitude. How could I not? We were not damaged. Our home was untouched. Nothing was smashed. Just my possessions were removed. I can cope with that, I convinced myself. I will see miracles, the rav told me. And I did, but first I cried; tears flowed from a deep place within. A part of me had been taken; intertwined in the physical me. And then I saw the miracles and I came to understand. We remained, while what was not needed was taken. It was up to me to start over, to realize that Hashem gives and Hashem takes. His infinite wisdom decides what I need and what I do not need. It was up to me to accept, to forgive, to forget and start again. And I did, but this time with a different vision.

Today a few clothes hang behind a closed wardrobe door; they don't define me. It's the many thousands of words that dance out of my fingers and appear on the computer screen of my new basic computer that I cherish alongside my role as a wife, mother and homemaker for my precious family that will be mine for eternity. They will never be his, the robber's, who thought he had taken a part of me.

When I write things out I feel refreshed, I feel closer to G-d, I feel ready to embrace a new day.

# 12

I have a few ways I like to record special moments with my family. By nature I am a creative person. Since I was a child I penned stories and used my love of taking photographs to capture things that inspired me. Photographic images, although silent, are a very effective way to remember and tell a story.

Throughout the early years of my marriage, when everything was so fresh and exciting, I made a real effort to safeguard my memories with stories and photographs. One day I know I will cherish these mementos; many of them have inspired some of my favorite published stories. Many of them have helped me remember how priceless every moment was.

I wrote this story in my journal after experiencing the first rain of the season with three of my children when I was expecting my fourth. I receive a lot of *koach* from my children; they see everything new with such enthusiasm, which in turn invigorates me. When my boys experience something for the first time, their wonderment stuns me and always inspires some sort of grateful or creative response.

The Torah tells us that what was so special about Aharon Ha-kohen, the brother of Moshe Rabbeinu, is that every time he did a mitzvah, it was as if he did it for the first time; his enthusiasm was on the level of his first experience.

Children live in the moment. It is a place where I have learned to feel most comfortable and most alive and most appreciative. When I unexpectedly dream of the past or the future, I feel weighed down by that movement. To reconnect with the present, I simply focus on where my children are holding. This motion centers me in the here and now; what a breath of fresh air!

I love reading this journal piece; it is meaningful to me for lots of reasons but mostly because it celebrates living with my children in their world today — and what a gift from G-d that is.

## The First Raindrop

We went to the park yesterday. The weather was brewing up a little storm. Perched on top of a hill amongst pine trees the boys ran around and slid down slides amidst new wind and old sand. Our hands became useful shields against the particles that filled the air and in the end, tired and dust covered, we made our way home down the steep hill.

In the beginning the children's resentful steps moved slowly until I managed to capture their interest.

"Look at that huge wintry white sun," I said with genuine surprise. It really was a new sight for the New Year.

"It's so big! Perhaps if we reach out, we'll be able to touch it, Mummy," said my *bechor*, Yitzchok Simcha.

"How interesting; the summer sun looks so different from the winter sun," I said. "I love the pretty sky. What colors do you like?"

"I love the pink and orange," my second son, Aharon, said, smiling up at me.

"Me too; I also like the red," said Yitzchok Simcha.

We were on our way.

"I also see gray clouds, Mummy — I think rain is on the way," Aharon announced, looking up with concern in his eyes, which had to be shaded again.

A gust of wind had brought us all to a halt. The baby carriage hood had been pulled neatly down, but Mayer Zev, determined to join in, pushed it back with a giggle and outstretched his hand trying to touch the quickening changing shades of the late afternoon.

"I think it's time for a song," I said, energized by the dynamic winds and expansive sky. One could see at least five pine-covered mountains from where we were standing on the empty pathway, devoid of people and cars.

Within seconds we were singing *Mashiv Haru'ach* at the top of our lungs, trying to compete with the noisy wails of wind and making rhythmic up and down motions with our feet; a sort of jig as we went.

"This would make Daddy laugh," I said. "He's always the first one to inject a touch of song and dance into any situation." I gave my boys a kiss on their heads.

In the night, I heard them and I felt happy; the first raindrops on my beloved Yerushalayim.

"You see, Mummy, Hashem heard our *tefillah*," was Aharon's second sentence after *Modeh Ani*, and after he had rushed into my room to give me a weather report.

I decided to leave the house twenty minutes earlier than the Bayit Vegan bus we take to get Aharon to *cheder*. I wanted to take a walk. I wanted to experience the smells and the sights after the first rains — we had just had eight months of uninterrupted good weather and blue skies.

When Aharon saw the first new puddle of the year he stood still and peered into the water.

"It's like a mirror, Mummy," he said.

I looked down at a stunning picture of the bright sky and streaky white clouds reflecting back at us. The mirror was "adorned" with autumn shades of leaves of various sizes; large and small in muted pastel pinks and bright yellows.

"It's too precious to walk through," I said.

Aharon nodded, then took my hand and we walked around "her" toward the *cheder* gates.

"We can use our noses to inhale the rain air. Today it's so pure and clean," I taught my son.

As we stopped to do just that, memories of winter walks through the English New Forest — one of my most favorite places outside of London — veiled my eyes.

We then passed a cluster of trees, each moving to its own internal music. I thought that maybe the tips of the branches might be expressing their personal praise and thanks to the Creator for the nourishing rains.

I, too, felt appreciative for many reasons. The most important was that I was having an opportunity to return again to the beginning; I felt so young, so inquisitive, so very in touch with the world around me and it felt good.

I looked down at Aharon, so small and so new to the world.

"I am loving this walk, Mummy," he said, clutching my hand a little tighter.

"So am I, my *ziskeit*," I said, smiling down on his adorable, content face.

I hope my son will remember this feeling, this moment, when he walks with his own child one day, and that he recognizes the connection between his yesterdays and his relationship with me. And when he walks with his own child I hope he will remember me, who loves him so dearly and wants to show him the beauty of life through loving the moment, just as he lives it.

# 13

In summer of 2004 our fourth son was born. By this time I had moved from *Hamodia* Magazine and was working for *Mishpacha* Magazine, a Jewish Family Weekly.

I had joined the launch team of this new magazine in the spring of 2004. My *Mishpacha* column was called "Daughters of the King". It featured interviews with Orthodox Jewish women worldwide.

I loved writing this new column; each week I talked to women in Jewish communities around the world, who told me their stories, which in turn enriched my own life. Everywhere I went I looked for women to interview; everyone I spoke to was a link to a new woman to meet. My world suddenly became a very interesting place; the column was popular because people said each story was an inspiration for their own lives and helped them to help others. People liked to talk to me and give me interview ideas and tell me a little of their own stories.

At this time my life became very streamlined and compartmentalized — it had to be like this so I could meet my personal and professional goals.

My typical daily schedule looked like this:

5 A.M. until 8 A.M. — children's time before they left for *cheder*. Time when I made the beds and put up the laundry and organized the meals for the day.

8 A.M. until 1 P.M. — writing time.

1 P.M. until 6.30 P.M. — children's time in the home, our small

garden, the park, the zoo or out and about doing errands to-gether.

7 P.M. — midnight or through the night, when I was working on a feature series, which demanded overseas telephone interviews.

One or two mornings a month — errands for the family.

Every day there were special get-togethers with my husband, generally at 8 A.M. and 10 P.M. for twenty minutes or so, usually over a cup of tea and a piece of cake. Shabbos, Chol Hamo'ed, and *bein hazmanim* were our family quality time.

When I started writing full-time, my husband offered to take on the weekly food shopping; he has developed a talent for shop-ping economically. I feel proud that my husband does this job; it's his way of doing something positive for our family. When he ar-rives home with food parcels the children are so excited and ready to help put things away.

This type of family life and work schedule doesn't fit everybody. It suited me because my husband wasn't home for long periods of time except late at night. *Bli ayin hara* he spent (and still spends) every possible moment in the *beis medrash* learning Torah or teach-ing students privately. What fascinates me about my husband's learning is the more he learns, the more he sees there is to learn and the more humble and impassioned he becomes.

So, while I am writing and praying for *siyata d'Shmaya* to par-ent our children, manage the home, and be a good wife, I some-times think of my mother's admirable housekeeping and I strive to emulate her. I may not have the budget she had, but I am compen-sated with the knowledge that my husband is learning and enjoying what he is doing and we are happy for each other.

While I know many people don't thrive creatively when they have to initiate their own work agenda, work by e-mail with an overseas office, or work in isolation most of the time, I do well in all these situations because I have trained myself to focus on one thing at a time. I am the happiest when I am left alone to get on with what needs to be done. When I am with my children, they are the priority, when I am writing, that is the priority, and so on with everything I do; I find a 100 percent focus on any given task works well for me.

What challenges did I face while I worked for *Mishpacha* Magazine? The main one was that I was tired most of the time, but not a lazy tired; it was an exhausted, "satisfying" sort of tiredness from hours of research, interviewing and writing in between all the other obligations of my day, so when bedtime arrived I was physically relieved, but so very happy and fulfilled. When I write I tend to forget I am a person; it's only when I stop writing, as tiredness suddenly overtakes me, that I suddenly remember I am a person and I need to sleep and look after myself.

Writing has this angelic effect on me; it takes me out of myself, beyond myself, to a place where I feel so close to G-d, I forget myself and don't think of the mundane (and if I do, for a split second, the task to be done is promptly noted on a yellow legal pad by my keyboard and I continue unaffected, knowing I will get to it at the right time). Even though this all sounds rather euphoric — and Divine — when I worked for *Mishpacha* I lived a very responsible and organized life, very much in reality earning the *parnassah* for my family and working the hardest I have since I worked for Independent Television News in my mid-twenties; I wrote a weekly column and was working on at least one or two features all the time. I felt blessed to be doing something I loved for Klal Yisrael.

After two years *Mishpacha* discontinued my weekly column for women. After this — even though I continued working for *Mishpacha* and they were happy about this — my heart wasn't in my writing and this bothered me very much, so I started to research ideas on how I could continue writing for women in the way I knew best and I felt the reader loved best.

In April 2006 I heard whisperings that a new women's magazine was being established and my heart skipped a beat as I was in the midst of researching my own idea of this kind. By June 2006 I was features editor and features writer for *Binah* Magazine, a new magazine for Jewish women.

It wasn't easy for me to leave *Mishpacha*. I loved my relationship with my *Mishpacha* readers; everywhere I went I met them and their loyalty inspired me. But I felt this move was the best option for me; it presented an opportunity to give of myself exclusively to women readers. Sometimes we have to move on to move up. Moving up doesn't necessarily mean that what we left behind wasn't good enough anymore; moving up means moving upwards in our *avodas* Hashem.

At *Binah* Magazine we started from square one and slowly but surely we are building a great magazine with a loyal following.

Each day I wake with much gratitude to G-d, my supportive and encouraging husband and my excellent editors and the professional editorial team in New York, our head office. Each day I write for the women of Klal Yisrael and I love it.

# 14

If I had to narrow it down, here is what make life precious for me.

1. My need to feel G-d and the knowledge that I do when I am writing for Klal Yisrael and helping women on their journey of life.
2. My family's love, approval and encouragement and my beloved children.
3. Private, quiet time to think, breathe and rejuvenate, which I do by going to the beach often and sitting in our garden or taking walks in the forest behind our home.
4. Shabbos *Kodesh*.

I really love Shabbos now and prepare for it all week long.

When I think about how many Saturdays I wasted in my youth due to my own ignorance, I feel ashamed; how I spent the day doing things that added nothing to my life that had a lasting effect.

I experienced my first Torah-true Shabbos — after my return from India in 1992 — at the home of Rabbi Rashi and Ruth Simon in London.

By the time I was invited to the Simon's Shabbos table I had already read a little bit about Shabbos observance and the *halachos*. Yet what I actually experienced was not written about in books.

On Shabbos the living room looked beautiful. Ruthie arranged lovely flowers beside the polished Shabbos *licht*. The white-cloth adorned table was elegantly set with delicate china and pretty napkins and silver flatware. The food was scrumptious; each serving fresh and tasty and to the liking of each member of the family because Ruthie cared about everyone's fancies. The children were lively, sweet, well-behaved when they wanted to be; gaining their parents' respect and time meant something important to them. The Simons involved their children in the conversation giving them good old-fashioned attention: smiles, a good word, a kiss on the head, a hug and tender loving care for their efforts. The discussions centered on Torah thoughts from the *parshah* as well as what the children had learned that week in *cheder* or school. The interchanges made for an animated, unusual meal. I went home fully satiated intellectually, spiritually, emotionally and physically.

Shabbos was a wonderful discovery; I had never experienced anything like it in my life. I wanted to have a day like this every week also. Why not? I was a Jew and Shabbos was created for me.

Making the choice to keep Shabbos wasn't the challenge. The pressure to do what everyone else did on Saturday and the feeling of exclusion when I decided not to join the fray was my challenge. But I moved my favorite pastimes to Sunday and sooner or later I had to make new choices because some of those pastimes were not appropriate for me anymore. Exercising race horses and polo ponies was one of them. But my love of horses doesn't stop me from loving Shabbos and keeping Shabbos today.

Shabbos involved learning a lot of laws; I learned them by reading books. I remember my silliest mistake made out of sheer ignorance. I used to meet Rabbi Simon at the shul at the end of our street for *Kabbalas* Shabbos and then walk home with him to his home for the Friday night meal. I would rush home from work, quickly change into something appropriate for Shabbos and then race up the street to be on time for *Lecha Dodi* — the prayer to usher in the Shabbos at sunset.

One *erev* Shabbos it was raining cats and dogs, as they say in England. After Maariv, I claimed my coat and umbrella and went downstairs to meet Rabbi Simon in the foyer. He was donning his Shabbos coat and hat, as were all the men, about twenty at the time.

"Don't worry," I said. "We won't get wet; I have my umbrella."

I will never forget Rabbi Simon's face; he smiled sweetly, not saying a word and as I came closer he said in the softest, kindest voice, "Leave the umbrella here; we don't use this on Shabbos. It's okay; it's not far to our house." And off we went.

I didn't feel reprimanded, just educated in the nicest possible way. I collected my umbrella after Shabbos and didn't mind at all getting wet. The evening that followed was worth the inconvenience of being a little damp during the delightful meal.

Shabbos in Israel is also something special because — where I live — everyone is doing it with you, unlike in London where you have to pass cars and people in their regular mode of living like any other day.

In late August 1993, after a few weeks in Jerusalem, spending Shabbos with families who were welcoming and good company, I went with one of my dorm friends from Neve Yerushalayim to a Jewish community outside of Jerusalem for Shabbos.

I will never forget my first Shabbos on a *yishuv*; it made an indelible impression on my soul. The journey to the *yishuv*, which was nestled in the Judean Hills, took about one hour from Jerusalem, a ten-minute drive from the town of Efrat. We stayed at the home of an American doctor and a Dutch teacher. They lived in a simple trailer with a vegetable garden (until they had saved enough money to build their own house on their plot of land they owned on the *yishuv*). Their hearts and souls were anything but simple; they were deeply spiritual people and masters of *hachnasas orchim*, looking after guests.

We unpacked and had a light meal of fresh humus and crisp garden salad, hand-picked by our hostess Chana who then took us on a walking tour of the *yishuv* of a hundred American and Israeli families. The view from every vantage point was miles and miles of rolling hills dotted with olive groves. The light was splendid; the dusk was arriving and the hills were tinged with a ray of warm colors, mostly lilac, pink and faint gold.

After watching Chana light Shabbos *licht*, we went to shul, an aesthetically-pleasing hand-built wood and stone structure on a hill in the center of the *yishuv*. As we entered the women's section of the shul, we were greeted by the women of the community who were dressed in long, flowing, flowery dresses and cream fabric or lace headscarves.

"They look like they have just walked out of the Bible," I said to Chana.

She smiled, adjusting her own white lace headscarf.

"This is how Sarah Imeinu must have dressed," I said.

Shabbos clothing in London was fashionable, elegant suits. I had never felt comfortable in this attire which was also the dress code for business.

"These women look so lovely and feminine," I concluded with a touch of regret. I envied their freedom to dress in such a way. They did not wear the traditional *sheitels*, wigs, worn by the *Litvishe* community, which I didn't favor for myself. For them fabric scarves tied attractively was their choice for expressing the mitzvah married women perform when they cover their hair.

Soon the shul filled up. I pressed my face to the lattice *mechit-*

*zah* to get a glimpse of *yishuv* family life; the fathers and sons wore white shirts, white or beige pants and white knitted kipp*ot*, or traditional *Chassidishe* dress (*bekeshes* and fur *shtreimels*).

Fathers and sons talked excitedly in learning; a familiar hum resounded that reminded me of the day I stood in the women's section of the shul in Meah Shearim on a visit from London with my parents when I was fifteen years old.

When the *tefillah* began I felt goose bumps all over: the singing was so sweet and pleasing I started to cry. It was if my soul recognized the melodies.

The dancing after *Lecha Dodi* was modest yet lively; the energy was spirited and joyous. The vision of white apparel and happy praying and dancing souls was mesmerizing.

"I hope Heaven is like this," I said to my roommate, as we held hands and danced with the women hidden behind the lace curtain separating us from the men.

As we moved in circular motions, a memory from the past flicked through my mind. When I was a teenager, in Israel for the first time after my brother's bar mitzvah, I had wondered what transpired in an Orthodox shul in Jerusalem behind the lace curtain. Now I knew a little more about the mystery of the lace curtain and the mystery and the beauty of my tradition which was coming alive for me in the most enchanting way.

The following week I spent Shabbos with a *Chassidishe* family in the Kiryat Sanz section of Netanya, a one-and-a-half-hour car ride from Jerusalem; this was my first time meeting a Chassidic family. Har Nof is a predominately *Litvishe* community, as is the *derech* of Neve Yerushalayim.

We arrived in Kiryat Sanz in the early afternoon. The hostess greeted me at the door wearing a pastel-colored, turban-style head covering and a pastel floral housecoat. The husband was wearing a black silk coat and a *shtreimel*. I was enchanted by this couple, who had the appearance of royalty. Their ways were modest and the way they lived their Torah life was careful and radiated something new and appealing to my senses. Their daughters acted by example; they were soft-spoken and modest.

In shul on Shabbos morning I noted that each woman carried herself like a princess. The women prayed and conducted themselves in a refined and feminine way. The fathers and sons had the appearance of princes; well-groomed and modest but regal in stance and conduct.

I stayed an extra day with the host family, Americans who had settled in Israel many years previous, as I felt so comfortable in the community of Kiryat Sanz. It was different from the *yishuv*; even though Shabbos was Shabbos wherever I went, the way communities and families in their homes experienced Shabbos was very different. I could see myself living in Kiryat Sanz and, funnily enough, it is the one place we have been going as a family twice a year since we married eleven years ago.

*Erev* Shabbos is the day I say "stop the work week it is time for me to get off" as I prepare the home and the food *l'kavod Shabbos Kodesh*; when I am lighting *licht* I can feel my soul rejoicing as my body relaxes and my senses shift as I enter my highest dimension of living with G-d.

Where I live, there are no cars on the road and the silence is a pleasure. And everyone you see outside is dressed in Shabbos clothes, which makes for a lovely community atmosphere.

I feel Shabbos in our home is the most special twenty-five hours of the week. We prepare for its arrival in small ways every day of the week and especially so on Thursday and Friday. The house is cleaned, all the laundry is done, challah is made, food that each of us enjoys is prepared, fresh flowers are bought and arranged nicely, and sometimes guests, *bachurim* or families are invited so we can share Shabbos *Kodesh* in our home with others.

When we don't have guests, our time is given exclusively to our children; Shabbos is crucial bonding time for "Daddy and the boys". Shabbos morning, after my husband returns from *vatikin*, he has a hearty Shabbos breakfast with the children and then takes them to hear the *leining* in the Boston shul, so they hear the *parshah* and then to the Bostoner Rebbe's *tish* in his home and then usually onto a *kiddush*. In the afternoon he takes them to a Tehillim group and makes time to learn or talk to each child about his week in *cheder* or *gan*. They join the rebbe for *shalosh seudos*, third meal of Shabbos, in shul; a most lively and happy occasion every week — with singing, dancing and *divrei* Torah.

*The Bostoner Rebbe, shlit"a (center) a wonderfully inspiring
and happy role model, and community leader.
(Picture Courtesy of Neil Peterman of Har Nof; with sincere thanks.)*

I love seeing my family return from Havdalah with the rebbe; their faces radiant, a song on the tips of their tongues, a tap in their walk — all of which enhances the week ahead for all of us.

When I stop to observe my husband with our boys on Shabbos, I feel a greater love for G-d. When I see them singing together, learning Torah together, talking about their week and their lives, I think it was worth leaving behind the secular world for this — this is so beautiful and so right for each of us.

Sometimes when my husband is singing on *leil* Shabbos, and the children join in, I feel immense gratitude to my husband for making me his wife, and I feel immense gratitude to G-d for bringing to me to this life, this life which is so good for my soul.

# 15

Our Shabbos guests help us share the wonders of our life and help us see G-d in our daily lives.

I am usually the one who does most of the talking with the *yeshivah bachurim* after the main course has been served; my husband prefers to sing and learn with our children and then the *bachurim* and then to sit back and watch me answer any of the questions they fire at me — if and when the appropriate circumstance arises I tell them I am a *baalas teshuvah*.

With my husband's *haskamah,* I am ready and waiting with the answers. One question that comes up time and time again is the struggle to give up a career with money prospects for a life of learning Torah and a more limited income. The single boys are very eager to know the wife's perspective; they want to understand the mindset of someone further along the path of life than them.

This is my favorite topic because both my husband and I grew up in affluent homes — my husband in a *shomer* Torah and *mitzvos* home (with its source from generations way back) and myself in a traditional Jewish secular home — and now we live an Orthodox Jewish life on a very simple budget that combines my husband's *kollel* stipend and my earnings from writing features.

I tell the *bachurim* as it is; the whole truth and nothing but the truth, so they can consider their own options more thoroughly.

In the beginning, I found it challenging to live on a meager budget, especially when the children started to come along. I worried all the time about the future because I couldn't see us bringing in any more than we were now and we were a growing family. My parents' constant worrying about our struggle for financial security used to reduce me to tears. Seeing others who seemed to have more than us, who lived a similar Torah ideal, caused me to shed more tears. I was always grateful for my parents' gifts. And after our wedding I always appreciated my mother's "gift packages" of silver polish and essential items for all of us and sometimes something pretty for me to wear from Marks & Spencer, a store I grew up loving as a child and young adult and wished we had in Israel and I had a lifetime of unlimited credit.

And then we experienced a series of what I would term miracles, and slowly my faith and trust in G-d increased, and as it increased more and more I stopped worrying about money and put my trust in G-d; surely He would give us everything we needed, and if we didn't have something it was because He didn't think we needed it.

I tell over these stories often to our guests and our children because they give me spiritual strength and clarity. Ultimately for me, they increase faith and trust in G-d's way.

When I moved onto Brand Street as a divorcee, I had just one mattress to call my own, a gift from a friend. As my work as an art teacher picked up I was able to buy items one by one for the apartment. My books were all stocked on three bookshelves worth, about $30 each at today's rate. When I married the same shelves stocked my husband's books. His books were put in front of mine and they stuck out a bit. There wasn't a day that didn't go by when I would walk past these simple, useful bookcases and wish I had money to buy something more appropriate and befitting for my husband's large collection of *sefarim*.

This feeling niggled at me every day for about seven years until I stood in front of the bookcases and said, "G-d, I accept these bookcases just the way they are." And from that moment I decided my goal would be to accept G-d's choices for me, including His choice of furniture.

The next *erev* Shabbos I got a phone call from a friend who said she had left her husband and asked if she could come for a Shabbos meal with her daughter. I said she was most welcome to share our simple fare and we awaited her arrival after I benched *licht*.

I don't think I need to explain how I was feeling seeing her in her distraught state on the verge of something I had experienced myself nine years earlier, albeit without a child. My heart went out to my new friend as we tried to make her and her daughter comfortable.

On Sunday morning she called me to thank me for the most welcoming *leil* Shabbos.

"Leah, I couldn't help noticing your bookshelves," she said. "I imagine you live on a limited budget."

"Yes, *baruch* Hashem, it's best for us. This way there's less pressure and more acceptance of what we do have," I said.

"Well, I have a ten-door bookcase unit I would like to give you because I have to move this week and I can't use it for the time being and I don't know what to do with it. Would you take it from me and keep it until you can pay me a little something for it?"

I looked at my white bookcases and then I looked out of the window at the skyline and then I smiled.

"Yes, that would be lovely. How can we get it here?"

The next piece of furniture I bought for my Brand Street apartment was a table and chairs. A friend phoned me in an excited panic, saying her neighbor had just got engaged; she was selling her brand new table and chairs, as the *chassan* had something already. This dear friend loaned me the $250 to buy the furniture.

In our new home we have had many special meals around this table. Once we had someone tell us, "Perhaps you should have something fancier." When this person said this to us, I was saddened for a moment because I knew we didn't have the budget and then I instantly recalled how Rebbetzin Shain's father felt about his Shabbos table and chairs, as recounted in her book *All for the Boss*. I told them the following: many special people have sat at our table and enjoyed our hospitality; all my husband's and my family and also Harav Chaim Pinchas Scheinberg *shlit"a*, who joined us for a private dinner to bless our new home; Rebbetzin Shain when I hosted a *melaveh malkah* for a hundred mothers and daughters for a charity; Harav Shmuel Auerbauch *shlit"a*, the son of Harav Shlomo Zalman Auerbauch *zt"l* and HaRav Shmuel Deutsch *shlit"a*, the Rosh Yeshivah of Kol Torah Yeshivah, when we made *sheva brachos* for my brother-in-law, a year after Abba passed away.

Each chair and each place at our table has a history to tell; I would never sell this table and chairs to anyone.

Last year a visitor in our home commented about our Shabbos table and chairs, which are getting on a little and perhaps we should buy something more befitting for a house of Torah. I said to my husband, if G-d wants us to have a new table and chairs for Shabbos and for our sons' bar mitzvahs — as we plan to host the meals in our home — He will give it to us. My husband agreed and that was the end of the conversation.

The next day we had a phone call from a very close friend of my father-in-law who lives in New York. He told us he was refurbishing his Jerusalem home and he wanted us to come over.

"We'd like to give you this Shabbos table and chairs," he said, showing us a black lacquer extendable dining room table with ten chairs.

My husband looked at me; he knew it was not my taste but he also knew that I would never turn down a miracle coming to us disguised as a gift.

When we got home my husband asked me what we should do.

"Take it, of course. G-d wants to give us a gift and now we will be able to host all the guests for the boys' bar mitzvahs."

We made arrangements for delivery.

"Are you sure, Leah?" said my husband.

"Yes, with a white Shabbos tablecloth we won't see the black and it's a lovely set. They really looked after it nicely."

"Leah, it's only a few months old and I know you don't like black. I know you like rich, warm colors."

"If G-d wanted to give us the money for a new table and chairs He would, but this is not what's happening," I said.

The next day Abba's friend called to say he had changed his mind about the table and chairs.

"It's all for the best," I said to my husband when I relayed the message. He looked a little shocked; probably as shocked as I felt, but we put our feelings aside, believing this was all for the best. We certainly had no control over this story.

Two hours later the phone rang again. This time my husband took the call.

"We would like to give you money to buy something of your own liking," said Abba's friend. "When can you collect the money? We leave for New York in two days."

My husband called me to the phone to relay the message; we looked at each other and laughed silently — this was just unbelievable. Was it possible G-d was listening to us and giving us precisely what we really wanted?

When I tell this particular story our guests look at me and my husband with their mouths open and a dazed look in their eyes, they can't believe it either.

"So, what are you saying?" asks Yaakov, the twenty-two-year-old boy we have come to love as a son. "If I want to learn Torah and marry a girl who wants me to learn Torah and we live according to our means, which will be a *kollel* stipend, we'll manage?"

"I don't know what Hashem has in mind for you, Yaakov," I say. "But so far, I see this to be true for our family. I feel our *emunah* and *bitachon* have helped us accept what Hashem has wanted to give us and what He decided not to give, as the case may be. I feel we have seen miracles since we got married. I am sure in the merit of learning Torah you also might also merit what we have experienced."

"Have you always thought this way?" Yaakov wants to know.

"No, there were times when we were living on a shoe-string budget and had very little in the way of money or food in the house. At times I had a hard time respecting my husband's decision to stay in full time learning — after all, he has been in learning since he was a teenager — when it would have been nicer all around to have a decent salary coming in. But I came to the conclusion that perhaps when we have little and just manage, G-d is testing us to see if we still love Him even when things are tough. For myself, I know I felt it was easier to love G-d when things were rosy and we had everything we needed. When I was suffering — because I wanted a little more, because I wanted to give my children and myself a little more — I had my moments with G-d, kvetching to Him in my own way.

"Of course, there are those who *daven* their hearts out when they are suffering but this usually occurs in dire situations. I feel a simple life is the best way; it's manageable and you can live without expectations but if G-d wants to give you a gift, you'll appreciate it more and then learn to appreciate Him more."

"Really? Is it really like this?" says Yaakov.

"I think so, yes. For us it is," says my husband.

"Pirkei Avos says, 'Rich is the man who is happy with his lot.' This is my favorite teaching; *halevai* I should be *zocheh* to live by it. Right now it is a lofty aspiration, which I try each day to reach for," I say.

There was a time in my life when I thought I would marry a wealthy boy and never have a worry in my life about money.

Ironically, I feel I did marry a very wealthy boy, a boy rich in his love and knowledge of G-d and Torah and *mitzvos*. I am actually a very wealthy woman today; I have everything G-d wants me to have and I feel G-d's love.

The next thing a person might want is a father who is a rich. And I have that also. G-d's wealth is unlimited; He can give me what He wants when He wants — there is no limit to what G-d can grant me.

*Rebbetzin Ruchoma Shain and me on the threshold of our first sukkah; our shadchan joined us for a Sukkos seudah every year — before she moved to America — to celebrate the time when she redt our shidduch. For four years Rebbetzin Shain was my "surrogate" Bubbie, best friend and mentor; she was the first person to teach me the value of the words "Rich is the man who is happy with his lot." This is an ethic I saw her live by when I was in her company.*

# 16

While I was at *Mishpacha* I received an invitation to teach writing for the first time. A new friend, Esther Heller, directed the Annual Tzfas Women's Writers' Conference. She asked me to come up to Tzfas for a few days, give a workshop and meet women writers. I was very excited about this idea, even though I was apprehensive. My ever supportive husband said he would watch our young children and prompted me to agree. I am so pleased I did.

Mentoring writers in workshops and privately has become a central activity in my life. In May 2005 I initiated the first Writers' Journey Seminar in Jerusalem, a day of writing workshops for new and experienced writers and women in the publishing world. I was shocked by the response; it was a well-attended event. I didn't realize there were so many women in the Jerusalem area so enthusiastic about writing for themselves and the public at large.

I love to visualize my aspirations. We are now in the fifth year of this event and I have organized a further four one-day events of a similar nature, summer and winter writing sessions. I say "we," because these initiatives are for women organized by women, women who are inspired to join me and share their expertise because they, too, wish to see these events become a reality.

To honor the Writers' Journey Seminars, I self-publish a collection of Jewish women's writings, a showcase of new, aspiring and popular writing talent for the Jewish woman reader. The *Writers' Journal* is marketed internationally. When I receive thank you letters from Australia, Canada, South Africa, America and England, for example, I usually get teary eyed; can it be possible this dream has reached so far?

Once I felt too shy and worried to tell people my dreams, now I work industriously to actualize them. I put this change of outlook down to thinking too often in my life that I wasn't good enough to make things happen, to be successful, to help others because I had nothing to offer. I thought people would laugh at my dreams and they would be lost forever. How wrong I was. Every Jewish woman has something of worth to offer. Every *eved* Hashem was created by G-d for a worthy reason.

The Tolner Rebbe *shlit"a*, Harav Yitzchak Menachem Weinberg *shlit"a*, who was my spiritual guide for three years said to me early on in our relationship: when a Jew gives a title to his purpose for Klal Yisrael he can achieve great things for *Hakadosh Baruch Hu*, for his purpose is an integral part of his *avodas* Hashem.

When my father-in-law died I made a commitment to *Hakadosh Baruch Hu* that I would write for Klal Yisrael, that I would focus my creative talents on writing stories that would inspire people on their life's journey. The Writers' Journey Seminars and the *Writers' Journal* have become an extension of this endeavor. To help a woman on her life's journey through the medium of writing is a challenging and exciting opportunity. When women tell me they earn *parnassah* for their families from writing books or magazine articles that I or one of the Writers' Journey workshop leaders helped them write, I am so happy for them; when women tell me their *shalom bayis* or *emunah* is strengthened through penning letters to Hashem for *siyatta d'Shmaya*, I am in awe of the power of the written word; when women tell me they work through life's challenges through journal writing — another way to communicate with G-d — I know what they are talking about. I do this, too.

# 17

*July 2006*

M y seven-year-old son asked me a very important question this morning at 6:33 A.M.

"Mummy, what is the most important thing in life?"

He and his brother were rushing around our living room table on their house tricycles. The two little ones were making color-coded piles of Lego on the carpet.

I looked at each child and then gazed beyond their child's play that had been in motion since my "early risers" had woken at 4:55 A.M. I saw the tall pine trees moving gracefully in the forest wind, our view from the windows at the far end of our living room. As I took in the scene of natural beauty: our home, our *makom* of Torah, our family life, our legacy for future generations, I considered my options.

Is the answer the one my husband's aunt gave me when I sat beside her bed a few weeks before she succumbed to cancer? "Leah, all that matters in life is your health. All the wealth in the world, all the beautiful jewelry in the world can't buy you life."

Is the answer the one my father taught me as a child and that has underpinned every conversation with him until this day? "If you have money you have everything."

After my father lost his wealth in his mid-forties, when I was in my early twenties, he said, "Now I have 'nothing'." I didn't understand what he meant—he had always had Mum, me and my brother—wasn't that enough?

Is the answer the one Abba once gave me? "Family is everything to me, Leah. It is my life." And this is how he lived: for his familial relationships.

I think all these answers are good answers. One undoubtedly cannot live one day without health. One undoubtedly cannot live one day without money—even a *pashute* person needs money to pay for his essential needs.

One undoubtedly cannot live one day without family—real family, or friends who feel like family as it explains in Proverbs: *"A friend is always loyal, a brother is born to help in the time of need* (17:17)." Without family or a friend in the world, a person cannot live.

Every person will have a different response to this question according to his understanding of the world and his own life experience.

When my seven-year-old son asked me what the most important thing in life is, I answered, "A relationship with G-d." I feel when you have a relationship with G-d, you have *everything*.

# 18

After a relationship with G-d, I have to say that my work as a writer and editor has become a central source of inspiration in my life as a wife and mother, which, in turn, continuously inspires my relationship with G-d. This cycle of inspiration — my striving to have a relationship with G-d and my need and desire to write, and thereby inspire others — helps me manage to live the life Hashem has created just for me.

When I write, I feel so happy, so connected to the Source Who inspires my words, Who grants me my words everyday.

When I write, I feel a proximity to G-d that I only feel when I am deep in prayer and this is not something I can do twenty-four hours a day; *dveykus* in prayer is something that I experience periodically; *dveykus* with G-d is something I feel all the time when I write.

I never feel lonely or alone when I write.

I never feel a lacking when I write.

I never feel that a word written is a wasted word because it brings me closer to the truth; that a life with G-d is the only life; that a life with Torah is the only life; that a life of faith and trust in G-d's ways is the only life and that G-d's choices are the best choices for me.

When I realized that a Torah life was the right life, I felt relieved and more at peace with myself in G-d's world.

I thank You, G-d, for everything He has given me and everything He expects of me and everything I am trying to do with the gift of writing He bestowed on me.

I thank G-d for my husband and children, for my friends and for the women whose lives I have touched with my writing and my love of writing and for the women who have taught me so much about life and giving.

# 19

Our home is for our family; it is also for the family of Klal Yisrael. It's the place I welcome women who want to share their heartfelt thoughts and the struggles in their souls.

A lot of women talk to me about the challenging transformation from a secular way of being to an Orthodox Jewish way of life. After the challenges of marrying a husband who is learning full-time are put aside, and then dealing with all the issues that arise with some parents' reactions — not all parents react this way — to the turnabout in their daughter's life, and after talking through the long list of challenges relating to becoming a wife and mother later in life, one of the frequent issues women want to discuss is how to maintain personal interests and creative pursuits as a *frum* woman: which are best and where to find the time to do it, or should one forget about them altogether?

From the many conversations I have had, I realize that many women think that they need to abandon everything from their "past" life — their secular life — to fully integrate into the Orthodox Jewish way of life. I do not hold by this all or nothing outlook; I feel there are many aspects of everyday living that can be integrated and used positively in an Orthodox Jewish way of life if done in the spirit of Torah law within the boundaries of *halachah* and modesty.

When I came to Israel I made a terrible mistake; I gave up watercolor painting and photography — great loves of mine since childhood — and didn't make time for journal writing, traveling, listening to music, swimming outdoors, walking on the beach and generally being in the company of worldly intellectually stimulating women. I got so busy with serious spiritual discussions and pursuits and working all hours to earn a *parnassah* to pay my way in Israel, I relegated everything else, not realizing such a move would be detrimental to my development as a human being and my love of life.

In effect, when I became a *baalas teshuvah*, I cancelled out the life philosophy I once held so dearly and replaced it with something new and largely unfamiliar. Since I was a child I had always strived to live life truthfully and passionately and had always wanted a life that was personally fulfilling and happy and I had wanted to share that joy with others. The frugal approach I adopted early on as a *baalas teshuvah* transported me to an alien place; to a place of very simple living and systematic routine in most areas of living — not such a positive state of being — for someone with my upbringing, personality and innate potential.

In the first few years of living in Jerusalem I erased an integral part of my being and outlook in the name of streamlining and a quest for spiritual truth. My love of the arts, the natural world, animals, my love of expressing myself in writing more openly, of wearing what I really want to wear, traveling and meeting new people and much more disappeared from view.

In retrospect, I feel it was short-sighted of me to remove from my life everything or anything that made me feel great about life and enabled me to give more to Klal Yisrael through my talents. I feel this must be true, because since I started putting some of the things I used to love back in the framework of my Torah life, a splendid thing has been happening; I am starting to love life more and give more to my husband, children and my readers, which I think is a fantastic turnabout of events after worrying that I would never reclaim that exciting feeling about life I used to have.

This evolving turnabout in my life perspective became accelerated in the last year due to a most unexpected turn of events.

In the nine months that followed June 2006 I had two unexpected miscarriages and spent most of the year in the house too upset and transformed physically to show myself to the world. I was too immersed in losing myself in my work to do anything else but love my children and love G-d for giving me my writer's life to maintain our *parnassah* and my sanity during this most sad chapter of life.

G-d does not tell us why He brings us enormous ordeals; but what I did ask myself was what could I achieve regardless of the bad, the disappointment, the pain. I chose to write incessantly, to reach out to my reader with my words, to rise up towards G-d through my *avodas* Hashem rather than disappear into a deep dark pit of despondency and grief. I didn't talk about my feelings with anyone — a big mistake — I felt too closed to do so. Instead, I wrote whenever I could and cried a lot.

I would like to share with you a piece of writing I wrote after my third miscarriage on 7th March 2007.

### It Is Time to Count My Blessings

It is 12:21 A.M. The sky is black and the air cool. I am listening to the night sounds; the low breeze of the air conditioner; faint murmurings in the corridor; and now a persistent ring of a phone that abruptly stops and then starts up again.

I hear footsteps approaching. The curtain is pulled back. Two bright-eyed nurses walk inside the space allocated to me, one carrying a bag of intravenous. The auburn-haired one carrying the bag asks me about the smallest child in the photograph I have pinned on the board behind the bed.

"A girl?"

I turn my head and look into my son's face.

"No. A boy, like the other three, *bli ayin hara*."

She lays her hand on mine.

"How do you feel?"

I look into her eyes; the words could flow forever but I am selective.

"*Baruch* Hashem, I accept what Hashem has decided. I'm okay."

The two nurses slip away like a moon behind a cloud to the next curtain to the woman in the bed next to mine. A machine is wheeled to the bed by the nurse with the fair hair. My ears pick up a familiar sound and suddenly a mask of deep sorrow descends on my face — there is no witness — only I feel it and Hashem knows it. I may never hear that sound again, the beat of a tiny heart. The sound is beautiful but it pains me terribly. I put my hands over my ears but it's too late. I feel sick from the sound now; I want it to stop.

Today I miscarried for the second time in nine months; today once again I am desperately seeking the good in the challenge of loss; today, once again, I am experiencing the loss of hope, the loss of opportunity, the loss of potential, the loss of a gift.

I don't ask why. I want to believe Hashem gives and Hashem takes and it's all for the good because Hashem is loving-kindness and it is impossible His act of taking can be anything but good. I want to believe everything He does is with kindness and for my own benefit. I want to believe, but the believing is also a challenge.

The echoes of potential new life fade and the room is quiet again except for the whisperings of new night sounds; the deep breaths and soft *tefillos* of my two roommates — the overflow of another department — who are in the transition stage of birth. I have to endure this chapter of their lives until it's time for them to go to the delivery room; I am amazed at the insensitivity of the person who put me in this room with these two women in labor but I am too weak to voice my opinion and accept this is also G-d's will — for some reason that I will never understand.

The moments turn to minutes which turn to hours. The night becomes very long as I wait impatiently for the women in labor to move on, for the bright lights to be dimmed and for sleep to console me.

What are the feelings in my mind as I hear these sounds of new life while my womb now lies empty?

Firstly, I am logical, technical. What has happened here is a one in a million situation — the fetus was malformed, not particularly because I am forty-three or because I have a mild blood coagulation condition.

"This could have happened to a woman of any age. You're healthy. There is nothing you could have done to prevent it," said the doctor who performed the determining ultrasound.

I sigh.

Okay.

I see.

What next?

There is movement in the room. The wheels of the ultrasound machine are set in motion again. The heartbeat of the baby in utero across the room brings me back into the reality of my situation. The rhythm of life force is strong and consistent. How miraculous are your ways Hashem.

I look at the clock: time is passing. I think about my life. I review the chapters before I met my husband nine years ago. I think about the fact that I didn't understand my place in the world until I became religious when I was twenty-eight and I want to cry, scream, shout. I want to go back in time to when I was seventeen. I want to marry then and be a mother — then — not now. I want to take back all the years I was lost, that I tried to find meaning in my work and found emptiness, that I traveled the world to find myself and found nothing, that I had conversations and relationships that led me nowhere, that I acquired possessions and property that weighed me down and restricted growth and closeness to truth. I want to go back in time and change everything. I want to have learned back then that being a Jewish daughter was a privilege and preparation for the real task in life — to be a wife, an *ezer kenegdo* and perhaps one day, a mother. I want to change my past so I could have fulfilled that destiny rather than have gone to the *chuppah* at thirty-four thinking my marriage would be one of companionship because one can't take motherhood for granted.

Oh, how I wish I could change everything and start again so I could say, here and now, that I did the right thing with the years Hashem gave me.

As I lie in the hospital bed I will myself to calm down, to take deep breaths, to realize Hashem knew what He was doing, that there has to be a good reason for everything that had happened to me until this moment.

I think about the word "acceptance"; it is easy to write. It is easy to say. The challenge is to live it, to understand its true meaning, to believe it and know that to accept will bring one closer to peace of mind and greater love of self, life and Hashem.

One of the women in labor is pacing the room now. I know that feeling of impending birth. I have held a newborn close to my heart and wept with joy, *baruch* Hashem. My husband and I have been blessed four times, *bli ayin hara*, even though we have now lost three times. A loss is just a memory when you are able to look at the gifts in your life.

The nightlight illuminates the color photograph of our boys. They are smiling at me. I love each of them dearly, with all my heart. Today is March 7, 2007. It is now 1:10 P.M. It is a time in my life to count blessings, to wake up to the reality of my life.

I am living in Eretz Yisrael, in Yerushalayim.

I am married.

I am a mother.

I am living an ideal and trying to do my best, day by day.

The past cannot be wiped away or changed.

The future is in the Hands of Hashem and my free will — the choices I make that He offers me.

Only the present moment exists and it belongs to me, not a seventeen-year-old but a forty-three-year-old woman who learned today that acceptance is the key to the next passageway in life. If I accept my situation today I will heal, be able to take the next step, continue my *tafkid* in this world, and along the way perhaps help another woman who is experiencing what I have just experienced. I could help because I have stood in her shoes more than once in my life and it is a lonely place when you don't have someone to help you, someone to stand by you before and after the loss, someone to make meals for you because you are too tired or not motivated, someone to phone you to see how you are doing, someone to listen to the words in your heart and in your mind, someone who doesn't disregard your loss because you have more children, but someone who respects your loss because it is a loss.

The night before I was admitted to the hospital to have an operation to take out my sick baby in utero — a professional decision that was made after consultation with a committee of doctors and approved by *daas* Torah — I received a gift via car service from a person who knew about my situation. The present was beautifully gift-wrapped and came with a card. There were only a few words in the card but they caused me to release a loud sob and cry to *Hakadosh Baruch Hu* from a place within myself that I have never felt before. The words were "Always with you;" a double message, hence my response. She was telling me something that I *know* has to be and I *want* to be the foundation of my *avodas* Hashem — faith in Hashem — that *Hakadosh Baruch Hu* is *always with me* no matter what or when.

I feel that this gesture of kindness from this woman with *yiras Shamayim* is the most precious gift I have ever received — and I thank her for taking the time to think of me and reaching out to me in my time of need. I was comforted by her words — they helped me to continue with steadfast faith in the choices Hashem makes for me and to believe that within each Jew lies the potential for greatness, for *chessed* that is far greater than man himself.

# 20

*Middle of March — two weeks later*

In the garden of the building where my beloved Rebbe lives, The Grand Rabbi, Levi Yitzchak Horowitz, the Bostoner Rebbe *shlit"a*, there is a pomelo tree. This fruit-bearing tree, about 12 feet tall, resembles a bush rather than a tree. Pomelo is grapefruit-like in color and texture but takes the shape of a gigantic pear (or *esrog*) — typically the size of a smallish watermelon when it is ripe, requiring two hands to carry.

For years and years I have passed this pomelo tree which stands in the centre of a hexagonal grass garden edged in morning glory, tiny roses, jasmine and honeysuckle. The tree, with its perennial dark green leaves, is artistically pleasing contrasted to the azure skies we experience a good ten months or so of the Eretz Yisrael year.

The pomelo tree bears its fruit before Pesach. When the fruit grow ripe they look splendid on the tree, the epitome of bountiful beauty in the country I love.

When each fruit is ready it releases and drops on the grass, awaiting collection. I have never seen a pomelo disengage, but I have seen it through all its stages, which I find exciting. Furthermore, when I see the expectant fruit lying on the lush grass, a smile rises like a bright sun on my face because there is something about a new fruit ready for eating that brings me much happiness.

I owe much gratitude to this pomelo tree but, of course, firstly

I owe the gratitude to *Hakadosh Baruch Hu* who created it and placed it in this garden. So many times I have stopped by the flower-adorned fence to look at this pomelo tree; doing so gives me renewed strength and inspiration. Without fail this tree has been nurtured by *Hakadosh Baruch Hu*, and without fail each year it has borne a bounty of fruit.

After being cooped up in the house for so many months and then finally in the hospital, I was thrilled when the winds were high and the rain was heavy a few weeks after my return home. I had a great need to walk outside and let "the wind blow the cobwebs out of my head," as they say in England.

Within ten minutes, my four children and I had put on raincoats and rubber boots and had taken our umbrellas and were marching down the street on our way to the supermarket at the end of this street to buy something fun — like pizza and ice cream — to brighten the rainy week and my intense, reflective mood.

We worked hard at making our spirits joyous by skipping and hopping through puddles in the downpour, singing songs we love, laughing and enjoying the invigorating outdoors — for walking in the rain as a family can be a wonderfully inspiring event.

As we came upon the Rebbe's building the sky lit up. As we stood with our eyes fixed on the receding valley — the view from this street — a crack of lightening flashed in the distance. My children were in awe of the great light and sound show *Hakadosh Baruch Hu* had put on for them, for we were the only people in the street and the children were thrilled to have *Hakadosh Baruch Hu*'s world to themselves.

As the children were watching the now-darkened sky, waiting for the next fantastic light, I looked on my "friend" the pomelo tree, soaked and swaying unperturbed in the strong winds. The fruits, four months shy of their true potential, were holding their own, firmly connected. As the sky illuminated once again so did the tree, which looked majestic and steadfast in the face of the turmoil. It was at this moment that I realized how much I have benefited from "my" pomelo tree and how much its cycle of life has enhanced my cycle of life with a sense of appreciation and stability.

I have named this pomelo tree "The Tree of Faith"; when I pass it I make a point of stopping to admire it. Often this brings on an impromptu gratuitous dialogue with *Hakadosh Baruch Hu*. Standing with my eyes closed and my hand holding tightly on the garden rail, I ask G-d to grant me the wisdom to live in this world with insight, strength and vision, to raise my children so that their lives will be lives of faith and gratitude and love for the One that bestowed on them life and bounty. I feel a life of faith, gratitude and love will help my children develop a deeply meaningful relationship with G-d and help them individually achieve their true potential in this world, regardless of the winds of change and turbulence that could unexpectedly try to disturb their connection to the Source of all Life and Faith.

Often, while gathering equilibrium and inspiration from looking at the pomelo tree, I think of the Torah of the Noam Elimelech *z"l*. This holy Torah scholar tells the story of a rope around the world and how a Jew should always be holding onto the rope because every day something or someone is bound to shake the rope and a Jew that is holding tightly will never be dislodged or feel insecure. The rope is an analogy to faith in G-d; if we diligently maintain and guard our link to the Source of all Faith, we will more readily be able to endure and actualize a life steadfast in trust and faith in G-d.

# 21

I tried all sorts of methods to get myself in the right frame of mind after the miscarriage. There was no way out of my obligations, even though I would have loved to stay in bed for a month and talk to nobody. I had a family to look after, a home to run. On top of that, I had a writing seminar to host in a few weeks time; I was expecting over a hundred women, and I couldn't cancel the event. I had the third *Writers' Journal* to release for sale. In the end, there was no choice but to hold my head up high, put a smile on my face, ignore the way I looked and felt and get on with life while holding on to the image of the pomelo tree and the Noam Elimelech's "rope of faith around the world."

*Baruch* Hashem everything that was scheduled somehow went smoothly and no one caught on to what happened to me and why I looked a little different than normal on that day; gaining 44 pounds was the by-product of the year's unfortunate medical trauma.

I asked the Gerrer Rebbe for a *tikkun* for the loss of the baby; I felt the miscarriage was G-d's way of saying He was annoyed with me. The rebbe said, "Isn't it enough you lost the baby? That is your *tikkun*. There is nothing to do but gain back your strength and carry on." I took comfort from the rebbe's words and from knowing the soul of the baby will always be mine, just like the other two.

As much as I strove to overcome my loss, to work through my emotions and the "to-do" list in front of me, as the weeks passed I felt the tension and pressure mounting and my *shalom bayis* waning. I felt my human spirit and femininity was becoming dull and downhearted.

How could I bring a ray of hope and sunshine into my life to enhance a new outlook now that the door to my childbirth years appeared to have come to a close?

For reasons I cannot articulate so fully I felt empty and purposeless; I know it sounds ridiculous. I was blessed with a family and a productive writer's life. But deep down I wanted to continue having children forever; the experience had been so wonderful and fulfilling for me.

Traveling again jolted me into a positive new mindset. I was fortunate enough to find a sponsor to fund a new initiative to visit cities where *Yidden* lived. I initiated an agenda whereby I would report on the Jewish aspects of the city and interview women in the community. *Binah* Magazine was excited about the prospect of new vistas opening up for their readers, but I think I was more excited. I felt sure this new idea would help me heal more quickly and bring me back to life. Since March 2007 I felt a part of me had died and I hated the feeling. I wanted to love life again now that G-d had granted me an opportunity to start a new chapter in life.

In November 2007 I went to Venice and London and had dinner with my parents and brother and his wife for my forty-fourth birthday. This was very special because we had not eaten together as a family since the Shabbos of my *bechor*'s *shalom zachar* in 1999.

In the spring of 2008, I was unexpectedly invited for four days to Russia, which was a fascinating experience. This was the birthplace of my great-grandmothers.

This past winter I went to four European cities.

My husband's support enables me to do this new work; I am

grateful for his encouragement. I return excited and motivated, but above all appreciative of what I have in Jerusalem and what I can do to earn *parnassah* for my family and to inspire a feeling of *achdus* in Klal Yisrael through my feature articles.

Traveling, being in motion, exploring new places, meeting new women with new stories to share — all this has infused me with energy, and given my lifework a heightened sense of purpose.

Reflecting on how I feel today, after having just returned from Europe, I am grateful that my life is rebalancing itself; that I am able to be an *eved* Hashem and still able to pursue my personal and professional aspirations and my husband appreciates who I am. I am thankful for this turnabout because less than two years ago I felt so vulnerable, that my life was in the balance, and I had no control over my destiny.

When the nurse wheeled me into the operating room that day on March 7 2007, to have my live baby removed due to medical complications that were life-threatening to me, she asked me why I had such fear in my eyes. I told her the doctor had painted a life and death situation for me; I told her I had written farewell letters to my children just in case something terrible happened to me.

Over the next ten minutes, while I waited for the surgeon, I saw my life flash by me in full color; I was petrified I wouldn't wake up from the anesthetic, that I would never see my husband and four children again, that I would never fulfill my lifework and my dreams.

**22**

*January 2009*

I feel excited. I am working on this book with my final editor, also a woman who loves to write and who has achieved great things with the talents Hashem gave her.

Rebbetzin Yehudit Solovetchik calls me. "Come to my grand-daughter's wedding this Wednesday," she says. "Bring the children."

I look out of my study window; we are being blessed with an uncharacteristically warm, blue skied week. The children would love to go to an early afternoon wedding.

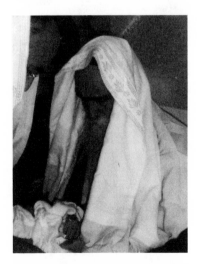

I prepare my children's Shabbos clothes for their arrival before they return from *cheder*. One child is coming home an hour earlier so we can make it to the *chuppah* on time. This is not something I do often, but Rav Dovid Soloveitchik *shlit"a* is my fourth and last son's *sandek*. I like the children to see their *sandek*. Our newborn son, like all our children, lay in his baby carriage

*Rav Dovid Soloveitchik, the sandek for our fourth son.*

289

beside Rav Dovid while he gave *shiurim* in his home, something I chose to do when the boys were born and something the Rebbetzin encouraged.

I have a plan for the afternoon but I don't tell the children; they adore surprises. We hop into a taxi and make it on time for the *chuppah*. Rav Moshe Sternbuch *shlit"a*, the Rebbetzin's brother, is at the *chuppah*. The children are thrilled. I allow my *bechor* to take photographs for the first time with my camera; he captures some stunning close-up photographs of our great Torah personalities, who he has the zechus to know personally. I am proud of his photographs that he shows me on the digital camera — and I tell him so. He smiles.

After cakes and soft drinks, we make our way to Harav Chaim Pinchas Scheinberg *shlit"a*, my rav, the *sandek* of my *bechor*; on Sunday my son will be ten. We enter the study and the children

*Appreciating a Torah way of life — for me — is seeing those that inspire and guide me on a regular basis and ensuring our children do also; the children with Harav Chaim Pinchas Scheinberg shlit"a.*

crowd around the rav for *brachos* and we take a photograph which will soon adorn the kitchen wall, where the children see chapters of their life framed in full color.

As pre-arranged, the children wait quietly in the hallway while I talk to the rav. I tell him the good news that we are nearing completion of my manuscript. I blush; nine more years has added more to the chapters of my life. I have no regrets; this is the time that I felt able and ready to finish it.

The rav smiles. "The story of how you became *frum* is going to be an interesting read for so many people." He laughs.

We have lived it together; there is not much he doesn't know. I remind the rav of this; he laughs some more and blesses me with continued *hatzlachah*, as he always does, and requests that I visit his rebbetzin, who is in the hospital.

That night, after taking my sons on to another wedding, this time the teacher of my six-year-old who is thrilled to arrive when the photographs are being taken and the *kallah*, whom he adores, invites him for a photograph with him alone, I call Rav Simcha Scheinberg, the rav's son, to ask about "Mamma." I am agitated, it's hard to fall asleep; I want to go over to the hospital now but I am completely exhausted from the long day that began the morning before as I worked through the night on the book manuscript.

At 8:30 A.M. I am pulling back the yellow print curtain in the emergency ward in Shaarei Zedek. I give the rebbetzin's helper, who slept overnight, a reprieve. She is relieved and so am I; I would prefer private time with the rebbetzin. She doesn't look like the same woman I met sixteen years ago. I sit beside her and take her hand and tell her I am here, that I love her and with Hashem's help she will be home very soon with the rav. She opens her eyes and tears well in the corners. Tears are already coursing down my face.

I cannot bear to see her age. I cannot bear to see her so vulnerable, so weak, so helpless.

I tell her about the weddings of the previous day, of my talk with the rav, I show her the photograph on my digital camera of the rav and the boys; her eyes flicker with recognition. I say Tehillim, begging Hashem to make her well so she can return to the living room in Mattersdorf I know so well, to her Lazy Boy recliner, to her beloved husband of seventy-nine years *bli ayin hara*. She is nodding all the while as I talk, and I tell her she might get well to get home for Shabbos *Kodesh* tomorrow night; she nods fiercely. She is coherent, even if she doesn't say much.

While she ebbs and flows in and out of "cat naps," I selfishly beg Hashem for a long life of good health, for sons like Rav Simcha who will care for me in my old age. I plead for no pain, no fear, and an easy journey until the end and I cry a river of tears while the rebbetzin sleeps and I watch the monitor beep and flash numbers.

I am happy to get home. To the present — not the past or the future — to the children who rush in all excited about a trip to the park next week with their *cheder*, to the mundane of washing up, preparing for Shabbos, to taking the boys out shopping to buy some towels for the house, to their swimming lesson and then home again, to Shema, to reading the working edit of a forthcoming feature at *Binah*, and then to editing the manuscript to meet the deadline.

I don't want to rush into the future tonight or race back into the past; the present moment is just fine for me.

And so, this snapshot of the moment is being lived in full color right now as I write these words which I decided would be the final chapter of this memoir, for now. Because one day in the future I will write more about the chapters of my life when I have experienced them, reflected on them and I am ready to share them.

I thank you, dear reader, for getting to the end of this story which I pray is just the beginning of another story, perhaps the story inside of you that is waiting to be written or shared with your family.

Leah Kotkes
Erev Pesach 5769/April 2009

# *Glossary*

**ACHDUS:** unity

**ALEPH-BEIS:** the Jewish alphabet

**ALTER:** (Yid.) older one

**AVODAS/ EVED HASHEM:** service/servant of G-d

**BAAL CHESSED:** person who performs acts of kindness for others

**BAAL (M.)/BAALAS(F.)/BAALEI(PL. M.)/BAALOS (PL. F.) TESHUVAH:** one/those who turn/s to a religious way of life

**BACHURIM:** single boys

**BARUCH HASHEM:** "Thank G-d"

**BAT BAYIT:** lit. "girl of the house," expression for a girl or woman who frequently visits a certain family

**BECHOR:** firstborn son

**BEIN HAZMANIM:** break between semesters in yeshivah

**BEIS DIN:** Jewish Court of Law

**BEIS MEDRASH:** Jewish study hall

**BEN TORAH:** lit. "son of Torah," one who dedicates his life to Torah

**BITACHON:** trust

**BLI AYIN HARA:** a blessing, lit. "There should be no evil eye"

**BRACHAH/BRACHOS:** blessing/s

**CHAREIDI:** ultra-Orthodox

**CHAS V'SHALOM:** Heaven forbid

CHASSAN: groom

CHASSIDISHE: chassidic

CHASUNAH: wedding

CHAZAL: our sages of blessed memory

CHEDER: religious school for boys

CHESSED: kindness

CHEVRA KADDISHA: Jewish burial society

CHUMASH: one of the Five Books of the Torah

CHUPPAH: canopy at a wedding ceremony

DAAS TORAH: Torah way of thought

DAVEN/DAVENING: pray/ing

DAYAN: Jewish judge

DIVREI TORAH: words of Torah

DRASHAH: speech

DVEYKUS: closeness, to cleave to

EIN OD MILVADO: There is none other beside Him (G-d)

EISHES CHAYIL: woman of valor

EMUNAH: faith

EREV: the eve of

ESROG: citrus fruit; one of the Four Species used on the festival of
   Sukkos

EVED/ AVODAS HASHEM: servant/ service of G-d

EZER KENEGDO: a wife, lit. "a helpmate opposite him"

EZRAS NASHIM: women's section in a synagogue

FRUM: religious

GABBAI: sexton

GALUS: exile

GAN: kindergarten

GET: Jewish divorce

**HACHNASAS ORCHIM:** hospitality

**HAKADOSH BARUCH HU:** lit. "The Holy One Blessed is He," reference to G-d

**HALACHAH/HALACHOS:** Jewish law/s

**HALEVAI:** if only

**HASHGACHAH PRATIS:** Divine providence

**HASKAMAH:** approbation

**HATZLACHAH (RABBAH):** (lots of ) good luck

**HEIMISHE:** Jewish hominess

**IR HAKODESH:** the holy city

**KABBALAS SHABBOS:** the prayer to welcome the Shabbos

**KALLAH:** bride

**KASHRUS:** kosher certification, the laws for keeping kosher

**KAVANAH:** concentration

**KEDUSHAH:** holiness

**KEVER/KEVARIM:** grave/s

**KIVREI:** graves of

**KIDDUSH HASHEM:** sanctification of G-d's Name

**KIPPAH/OT:** skullcap/s

**KITTEL:** white robes worn by married Jewish men on the High Holy Days and Passover

**KNEIDLACH:** matzah balls

**KOACH:** strength

**KOLLEL:** a place of Torah study generally for married men

**KREPLACH:** meat-filled dough pockets, traditional Jewish food

**LASHON HARA:** evil talk, gossip

**LEIL SHABBOS:** Friday night

**LEINING:** reading of the Torah in shul

**LICHT:** (Yid.) candles

**LITVISHE:** lit. "of Lithuanian origin," non-Chassidic sector of religious Jews

**L'KAVOD SHABBOS KODESH:** in honor of the holy Shabbos

**L'SHEM SHAMAYIM:** for the sake of Heaven

**MAKOM:** place

**MASHIV HARU'ACH:** lit. "He makes the wind blow...," part of the Amidah prayer

**MAZEL:** fortune

**MECHITZAH:** partition

**MELAVEH MALKAH:** meal eaten after Shabbos as a way of escorting the Sabbath Queen

**MESAME'ACH:** to make happy

**MEVATER:** to give in

**MEZUZOS:** ritual scrolls affixed to doorposts

**MINHAG:** custom

**MITZVOS:** Commandments

**MODEH ANI:** the prayer recited immediately upon awakening in the morning, thanking G-d for giving us back our souls

**NESHAMAH:** soul

**PARNASSAH:** sustenance; livelihood

**PARSHAH:** weekly Torah portion

**PASHUT:** plain; simple

**PESUKEI D'ZIMRAH:** part of the morning prayers that deals primarily with praising G-d

**PETIRAH:** the passing of

**RAV:** rabbi

**REBBI:** Jewish teacher

**REDT:** (Yid.) to suggest a match for marriage

**RIBBONO SHEL OLAM:** lit. "Master of the World," reference to G-d

ROSH YESHIVAH: head of yeshivah

SANDEK: person who holds baby during circumcision

SEFORIM: Jewish books

SEGULAH: Jewish ritual which brings blessing or good fortune from G-d

SHABBOSIM/OS: plural of Shabbos

SHALIACH: messenger

SHALOM ALEICHEM: lit. "Peace Unto You," traditional song sung at the beginning of the Shabbos night meal

SHALOM BAYIS: peace and harmony in the house

SHALOM ZACHAR: celebration held the Friday night after a baby boy is born

SHAMAYIM: Heaven

SHANAH RISHONAH: first year of marriage

SHEITEL: wig

SHEVA BRACHOS: lit. "Seven Blessings," the seven days of celebration following a wedding

SHIDDUCH/IM: match/es (as in marriage)

SHIR HASHIRIM: Song of Songs

SHIUR/IM: Jewish class/es

SHIVAH: the seven days of mourning following a funeral

SHLIT"A: "May he live to see good and long days"

SHOMER/ET/SHOMREI: observer/s

SHTETL: small Jewish villages in pre-war Eastern Europe

SHTIEBEL: small synagogue, generally Chassidic

SHTREIMEL: fur hats worn by Chassidic men on Shabbos and holidays

SIDDUR: Jewish prayer book

SIMCHAS HACHAIM: joie de vivre

**SIMCHOS:** happy occasions

**SIYATTA DISHMAYA:** help from Above

**SMICHAH:** rabbinical ordinance

**TAFKID:** mission; goal

**TALMID/IM:** student/s

**TEFILLAH/TEFILLOS:** prayer/s

**TEFILLIN:** phylacteries

**TESHUVAH:** repentance/return

**TZADDIK/IM:** righteous person/people

**TZEDAKAH:** charity

**TZITZIS:** traditional four-cornered garment with strings worn by Jewish males

**VATIKIN:** morning prayers, when recited at sunrise

**YAREI/'AS SHAMAYIM:** man/woman who fears G-d

**YESHIVOS:** plural of yeshivah

**YICHUS:** lineage

**YIDDEN:** Jews

**YIDDISHKEIT:** Judaism

**YISHUV:** Jewish settlement

**Z"L/ZT"L:** may his memory be for a blessing/may the memory of the righteous person be for a blessing

**ZEMIROS:** Jewish songs customarily sung at the Shabbos meals

**ZISKEIT:** (Yid.) "sweetie"

**ZIVUG:** marriage; intended marriage partner

**ZOCHEH:** merit

# About the Author

Leah Kotkes is the director of The Writers' Journey seminars and editor of *The Writers' Journal*. She is features editor and features writer for *Binah* Magazine. She hosts The Writers' Club, a bimonthly meeting in Jerusalem for new and experienced writers. She also mentors writers online.

Leah can be contacted at lifework@012.net.il. She is available to make referrals to Jewish woman writing mentors, writing teachers, and book publishers.

For more details and to read a few samples of her published material, which includes over 400 features, see her website: www.lifework.co.il.

For subscription or submission details at *Binah* Magazine contact: subscriptions@binah.com or submissions@binah.com.

# About the Final Editor

Gila Green is an award winning writer and independent editor. If you wish to contact her please see her blog: http://gilatal.blogspot.com or send her an e-mail: gilatal@gmail.com.